The Art of Wondering

The Art
of
Wondering

A Revisionist Return to the
History of Rhetoric

William A. Covino
University of Illinois at Chicago

BOYNTON/COOK PUBLISHERS
HEINEMANN
PORTSMOUTH, NH

Boynton/Cook Publishers, Inc.
A Division of
Heinemann Educational Books, Inc.
70 Court Street   Portsmouth, NH 03801
Offices and agents throughout the world

The following have generously given permission to use quotations from copyrighted
works:

Material reprinted from *The Complete Works of Montaigne*, translated by Donald M. Frame,
with the permission of the publishers, Stanford University Press. Copyright © 1943 by
Donald M. Frame, © 1948, 1957 by the Board of Trustees of the Leland Stanford Junior
University.

Material reprinted with permission of Macmillan Publishing Company from Plato, *Phaedrus*, translated by W. C. Helmbold and W. C. Rabinowitz. Copyright © 1985 by
Macmillan Publishing Company. Copyright © 1956.

Material from Lane Cooper, *The Rhetoric of Aristotle*, © 1932, renewed 1960, pp. 22–23,
91–93; excerpted by permission of Prentice-Hall, Inc., Englewood Cliffs, New Jersey.

Material from Cicero, *On Oratory and Orators*, translated by J. S. Watson (Carbondale, IL:
Southern Illinois University Press, 1970), reprinted with permission of the publisher.

Material reprinted with permission of the Macmillan Publishing Company from Giambattista Vico, *On the Study of Methods of Our Time*, translated by Elio Gianturco. Copyright
© 1965 by Macmillan Publishing Company.

In addition, parts of the author's previously published work were adapted for this volume,
including the following:

"Blair, Byron, and the Psychology of Reading," *Rhetoric Society Quarterly*, Fall 1981.

"Thomas DeQuincey in a Revisionist History of Rhetoric," *Pre-Text*, Summer 1983.

"Rhetoric Is Back: The Old and New in Critical Theory," *Postmodern Fiction: A Bio-
Bibliographical Guide*, Larry McCaffery, Ed. (Movements in the Arts, No. 2, Greenwood
Press, Inc., Westport, CT, 1986), pp. 217–28. Copyright © 1986 by Larry McCaffery.
Reprinted with permission of editor and publisher.

Library of Congress Cataloging-in-Publication Data

Covino, William A.
    The art of wondering.

    Bibliography: p.
    1. Rhetoric—History.   2. Knowledge, Theory of—
History.   I. Title.
PN183.C68   1988   808'.009   87-37561
ISBN 0-86709-193-2

Designed by Vic Schwarz.
Printed in the United States of America.
92   91   90   89   88   9   8   7   6   5   4   3   2   1

Contents

Acknowledgments

Parts of my already-published work on historical rhetoric have been revised and reassembled here. I am grateful for the permission to draw from: "Blair, Byron, and the Psychology of Reading," which appeared in *Rhetoric Society Quarterly* in Fall 1981; "Thomas DeQuincey in a Revisionist History of Rhetoric," which appeared in *Pre/Text* in Summer 1983; and "Rhetoric Is Back: The Old and New in Critical Theory," which appeared in *Postmodern Fiction: A Bio-Bibliographical Guide* (1986).

My thanks to Bob Boynton for his generous understanding and conscientious editing.

Nan Johnson was my best listener when this book was gibberish. And my wife Debbie, whose love and intelligence continually enrich my work, is the best of everything.

Introduction

Let him be taught not so much the histories as how to
judge them. That, in my opinion, is of all matters the
one to which we apply our minds in the most varying
degree. I have read in Livy a hundred things that another
man has not read in him. Plutarch has read in him a
hundred besides the ones I could read, and perhaps
besides what the author had put in. For some it is a
purely grammatical study; for others, the skeleton of
philosophy, in which the most abstruse parts of our
nature are penetrated.

Montaigne, "Of the Education of Children" (I: xxvi, 115)

I eschew all clear-cut interpretations.

Henry Miller, "Reflections on Writing" (179)

All teaching interprets history. However grand, this proposition seems true when we consider how the history of rhetoric
has been adapted by teachers and textbooks. For instance, until
recently, students and teachers were acquainted with an Aristotle
whose *Rhetoric* prescribed the style and arrangement of prose, and
whose *Poetics* reduced Tragedy quite neatly to rising and falling
action punctuated by catharsis. This was an Aristotle who had
reached us through centuries of interpreters, the Aristotle made
congenial to Medieval formulae for eloquence, Renaissance logic,
and Enlightenment positivism. This rather tidy, decisive Aristotle
was quite appropriate to mid-century American classrooms that

mimicked the military virtues that won the war and saved the peace: a codified, schematized philosopher who gave us *rules*.

The political and intellectual revolutions of the 1960s and 70s began to upset decorum in every quarter; re-evaluation of the teaching of writing provoked new investigation of the history of rhetoric, and the Aristotle who emerged and remains is more the relativist than the dogmatist, for whom invention is the primary rhetorical strategy. For this Aristotle, effective expression relies on preliminary exploration; he legitimizes "prewriting."

How we read the history of rhetoric, and what we read, and the implications for teaching we derive, can change. Peter Ramus and Hugh Blair and Thomas DeQuincey each invoke a different version of the rhetorical tradition; each implies a different pedagogy. In this century, Walter Ong and Robert Pattison each "use" Ramus to develop quite separate conceptions of literacy; and most recently, Cy Knoblauch and Lil Brannon straiten Aristotle and Cicero in order to negate the relevance of classical rhetoric to modern pedagogy.

The very instability of the "rhetorical tradition," its very indeterminacy, if you will, should alert us to the relationship among versions of history, conceptions of literacy, and teaching. While writing competency in the academy and the marketplace currently remains identified with formulary obedience, a "well-made box" (Weathers 6ff.), the importance of developing speculative imagination and critical inquiry, and the danger of valorizing communicative efficiency, are urgent issues. To challenge what the aims of discourse have become in a data-possessed, technocratic society, we can reconsider the history of rhetoric for alternatives to received ways of thinking, reading, and writing.

Postmodern criticism and philosophy have taught us to share Henry Miller's distrust of interpretations, to recognize further that all writing is interpretive: history or poetry or philosophy or journalism represses something in order to say something else. Surveying the history of rhetoric with a postmodern sensibility, this study advances two "repressed" propositions:

1. The major figures of classical rhetoric—Plato, Aristotle, Cicero—define and demonstrate rhetoric as the elaboration of ambiguity.

2. These figures anticipate more overtly renegade advocates of open discourse: Montaigne, Vico, Hume, Byron, and De-Quincey.

In sum, these "revisions" feature those who venture the primacy of shifting queries, multiple viewpoints, and formal innovation in rhetoric and writing: figures who have been either reduced to proponents of conventional rhetorical virtues, or scarcely noticed in the canon of historical rhetoric. A revisionist history raises the issue of revised pedagogy; I will conclude this study with some general propositions—"lessons of history"—for teachers.

The term "history" in the title may lead one to expect the usual, a neutral chronological exposition. Not so. Any reading of the history of rhetoric—which is, more precisely, a history of the texts of rhetorical theory—is partial; not only insofar as certain "episodes" are excluded, but also because the historian, the narrator, is always interpreting, bringing to the writing a special narrow-mindedness. You are warned, then, to read these chapters as provocation rather than information, as interruptions in the long-standing conversation about the elements of rhetoric.

CHAPTER ONE

The Classical Art
of Wondering:
Plato, Aristotle, Cicero

The tendency to summarize classical rhetoric with tree diagrams of finite categories and subcategories, or lists of rules and precepts, or unambiguous paraphrase, appeals to everything in us that would stabilize intellectual history.[1] Frozen portraits of the concepts of ancient rhetoric support the belief that they "have survived so vigorously the ravages of time and the usually inexorable processes of evolution" (Knoblauch and Brannon 22), that they are fixed monuments in the dust of progress. However, when we consider the history of intellectual history, in particular the history of rhetorical theory, identifying these "concepts of ancient rhetoric" becomes a problem, because they are consistently revised.

For example, the immediate contemporary response to Aristotle's *Rhetoric* was to add more system and substance. As Frederick Solmsen points out, "Aristotle's pupils and successors ... made it their object to fill out gaps which he had left ..., to arrange the material more systematically under certain basic categories, and to increase the amount of empirical data to be fitted into the framework of these categories" (279). Thus a sketchy theoretical statement was adapted to technical manuals and handbooks that replace the ambiguity and ellipses of the *Rhetoric* with more prescriptive and schematic treatments, which define the Hellenistic tradition, and which inform Roman rhetoric. An Aristotelian "tradition" that is maintained in some respects through Antiquity begins with a severe revision of Aristotle, a revision congenial to systematic instruction and the strict management of language that keeps emperors in power, a revision that both supplements and orders the original writing.

As Aristotle's successors demonstrate, reading rhetorical theory and constructing rhetorical history means construing new categories and systems of understanding. Richard McKeon reminds us that Boethius, who influenced the Western tradition well after his sixth-century work, "combined an Academic Aristotle, who taught the West to discuss invention and discovery, a Neoplatonic Aristotle who provided philosophical hierarchies for theology, and a Sophistic Aristotle who related philosophy to action and to literature" (715). The most resonant and famous revision of classical rhetoric, by Peter Ramus in the sixteenth century, is based upon Ramus's wholesale reconstruction of the history of dialectic, which he employs sometimes to express admiration for an Aristotle who validates Ramistic principles, and often to castigate an Aristotle who "has very greatly erred" (Howell 154). On the authority of his selective rendering of the *Organon*, Ramus reduces rhetoric to the study of style only and attaches topical invention and arrangement to formal logic. The appeal of a reduced rhetoric and a rigid logic, appearing near the dawn of the Enlightenment, is evident in "the huge market for books proposing various 'methods' and 'systems' and 'analyses' which flood over England as over all Europe from the seventeenth century on" (Ong 304).

For recent evidence, with a focus on the teaching of writing, compare the Aristotle born in the 1960s, the Aristotle of the "new rhetoric," with the midcentury Aristotle of the New Criticism. Rudolf Flesch represents the older Aristotle in his famous 1949 book, *The Art of Readable Writing*, which opens with a chapter titled "You and Aristotle":

> Chances are, you learned how to write—indirectly—from Aristotle. Look up the history of English grammar, composition, and rhetoric teaching; you'll find that it all started a couple of centuries ago when people first hit upon the idea

of teaching English-speaking boys and girls not only Greek and Latin, but English too. Courses and textbooks came into being; naturally, what was taught was simply Greek and Latin grammar and rhetoric, applied to English. Now since all Greek and Latin grammar and rhetoric go straight back to Aristotle (as any encyclopedia will tell you) and since the principles of English teaching are still much the same as they were two hundred years ago, what you were taught in school really comes down from Aristotle.

Take two rather striking examples, one from composition and one from grammar. In composition, probably the most important rule you were taught is the rule of unity. It is pure Aristotle—based on his famous principle that everything must have "a beginning, a middle, and an end." And in grammar the first thing you were taught was the parts of speech. Who first thought of parts of speech? Aristotle, again. So, whether you like it or not, you are an umptieth-generation Aristotelian. (1)

Done with his obeisance to Aristotle, Flesch argues that we forget the Greek: "There are several things wrong with using Aristotle as an English teacher today." First of all, Aristotle was not writing about English; second, Aristotle's rules applied only to three types of speeches and scarcely help with "advertising copy, promotional literature, press releases, and a thousand other" practical tasks. It is time, Flesch concludes, to "free yourself from Aristotle." He proposes "modern, scientific instruction" in writing, based on a "readability formula" (2, 9).

Flesch's introductory remarks are an explicit response to the history in which he is implied, to the recognition that he is an "umptieth-generation Aristotelian." He appeals to a history of rhetoric fathered by a severely prescriptive Aristotle, whose *Poetics* supplies composition rules and whose *Rhetoric* is valuable mainly for its discussion of style and correctness in Book III. Flesch revises the history pertinent to modern writing by setting aside a presumably ossified classical rhetoric, with all due respect, and appeals instead to the Age of Science, in particular contemporary experiments and data on reading and writing. He trades in an old history for a new one. Since the 1960s, a growing emphasis on invention and discovery in composition scholarship and pedagogy has recalled an Aristotle who provides "topics" rather than rules, and who illuminates discourse as too complex for reduction to the terms of positivist science.[2] And so we do share with Flesch the innovative effort to "free ourselves" from an Aristotle who no longer speaks to the present.

Influential appeals to a rhetorical tradition evince the tendency of all teachers to locate and "authorize" pedagogy with reference to a history. To the extent that any teacher is tethered to a concept of humanism which acknowledges contributions from Antiquity, all of us are "umptieth-generation" classicists whether we like it or not; we are the stuff of books and lectures, of our schools and our teachers and colleagues, of their schools and their teachers, of Hugh Blair's Quintilian, of Thomas Wilson's Cicero, of Theophrastus' Aristotle.[3] When DeQuincey says in his 1828 essay on rhetoric, "All parties may possibly fancy a confirmation of their views in Aristotle," he admits the importance and likelihood of appealing to a history of reference and notices the diversity of such appeals (*Selected Essays*, 83). DeQuincey suggests that the texts of the history of rhetoric are themselves "rhetorical," so that what they "say" varies with the context in which they are read, or "used."

Since Antiquity, the rhetorics of Aristotle and Cicero have enjoyed their greatest advertisement as the foundations of pedagogy, for student orators and student writers. As I have proposed, there are differences that distinguish the pedagogical use of classical rhetoric from age to age; however, a common emphasis prevails, upon rhetoric as *technique*. In the *Gorgias* and the *Phaedrus*, Plato opens the contest between philosophical and technical rhetoric, and technical rhetoric remains dominant through the centuries, so that the history of rhetoric is a continually stronger refutation of the suppleness of discourse, a progressive denial of the ambiguity of language and literature, a more and more powerful repression of contextual variables by textual authority. In ancient Rome, oratory was ossified into stock recitations and formulas; training in rhetoric maintained an elite class and contained the imaginative power that could threaten imperial rule. In the Middle Ages, God replaced the emperor; rhetoric instruction involved the correct,

established interpretation of scripture, as well as the severely formulary study of secular prose. When style became the substance
of rhetoric in the Renaissance, with questions of invention and
arrangement relegated to logic, learning rhetoric meant recognizing
and manipulating the ornaments of language. With the Cartesian
reduction of knowledge to "plain" observation from the seventeenth century onward, approved style became plain style, and the
primary virtue in both exposition and literature was perspicuity.
The Royal Society of London for Improving Natural Knowledge
moved to "reject all amplifications, digressions, and swellings of
style; to return back to the primitive purity, and shortness, when
men delivered so many *things*, in an almost equal number of *words*"
(Sprat 113). In 1840 DeQuincey explicitly leagued himself with a
forgotten rhetoric of ambiguity as he called for a return to discourse
that exploits uncertainty, the play of "inversions, evolutions, and
harlequin changes" that "eddy about a truth"; but, DeQuincey
concludes, "the age of rhetoric has passed among forgotten things"
(*Selected Essays* 97).

Techniques, rules, and formulas for composing and arranging
finished discourse fill the handbooks that comprise the mainstream
tradition. The "forgotten" rhetors are those who elaborate Plato's
conception of rhetoric as (I will argue) an art of wondering, and
writing as a mode of *avoiding* rather than *intending* closure. Aristotle
and Cicero have been forgotten insofar as their demonstrations
that persistent exploration is the substance of rhetoric have been
dissolved by "technical" explication. The technical tradition up-
holds the identification of Aristotle with reductive summaries and
diagrams and separates us from the Aristotle ranging among num-
berless possibilities, so evident in an untutored reading of the
Rhetoric. The Cicero we have inherited teaches formulaic oratory,
and the Cicero we have forgotten—the mature philosopher of *De
Oratore*—recalls Plato's *Phaedrus* as he evokes multiple perspectives,
disdains and mocks petty precepts, and leaves the debate over the
nature of rhetoric unsettled, inconclusive. The very fertility of both
the *Rhetoric* and *De Oratore* locates them in both the "philosophical"
and the "technical" traditions of rhetoric. Stressing how both
treatises advocate and illustrate rhetoric as philosophy, we recognize more fully their relevance to Plato's advocacy of philo-

sophical rhetoric and the contribution of classical rhetoric to a postmodern theory of discourse. Reconsidered, Aristotle and Cicero follow Plato, as they enfranchise a philosophy of composition that exploits rhetoric and writing as philosophy.

Plato, *Phaedrus*

Commentary on the *Phaedrus* writes a history of confusion. Since Antiquity, those engaged and seduced by the dialogue ask the urgent question, "What is it *about?*" As Reginald Hackforth admits in his introduction, "It is not obvious, at first reading, what its subject and purpose are, whether there are two or more, and if so how they are connected" (8). Josef Pieper recapitulates a "strange assortment of interpretations" to propose that "elucidation has run wild": since Antiquity, the *Phaedrus* has been called a treatise on beauty, or love, or the soul, or "the art of untrammeled thinking and of creative communication," or anamnesis, or community, or the philosophical foundation of the Third Reich (Pieper xii–xiii). The critical urgency to locate a unifying subject or purpose in the *Phaedrus* sets aside the irresolute complexity that informs philosophical rhetoric and writing for Plato. Reducing the conceptual and personal drama of this dialogue to academic summary follows the tendency to read philosophical rhetoric as a digest of information, as a taxonomy of instructions, and thus effectively discounts the striking ambiguity of form and meaning that makes philosophy (and rhetoric) possible and necessary.

Debate about the subject of the *Phaedrus* rests on the assumption that philosophical and literary "greatness" is accompanied by philosophical and literary unity and coherence. When these qualities are not obvious in a first reading, then one unwilling to challenge Plato's greatness must reread and search for them, as with Professor Hackforth above. Jowett's introduction to the *Phaedrus* acknowledges the presupposition that greatness and unity operate in tandem, then proposes that this dialogue is a special case:

> There seems to be a notion that the work of a great artist like Plato could not fail in unity. . . . But the truth is that Plato subjects himself to no rule of this sort. . . . He fastens or weaves together the frame of his discourse loosely and

imperfectly, and which is the warp and which is the woof is not always easy to determine. . . . [However] amid the appearance of discord a very tolerable degree of uniformity begins to arise; there are many threads of connection which are not visible at first sight. At the same time the *Phaedrus*, although one of the most beautiful of the Platonic dialogues, may be admitted to have more of the character of a "tour de force." (III, 368–70)

Jowett's discovery of "a very tolerable degree of uniformity" suggests that the difficulty of the *Phaedrus* originates with the limited tolerance of readers for its variegated warp and woof. Even this admirer of Plato's discursive license seems constrained to reify the text.

The established toleration of suspiciously fractious discourse, via the discovery of unity and its attendant virtues—clarity, coherence, closure—abates any controversy over the first-order prominence of the *Phaedrus* in intellectual history. But more important, for those of us who do agree that this dialogue deserves preeminence, the long-standing assumption that the *Phaedrus* is "great" and therefore "tame" forecloses our participation in the living and open inquiry that Plato is "about." Representing the practice of suppressing the discontinuities and ambiguities in the *Phaedrus* in order to understand it as the exposition of principles, Helmbold and Rabinowitz explain in their introduction that although Plato's "amiably discursive style" challenges critical appreciation, "in recent times judgment of the value of the dialogue seems to have settled down":

> Practically everyone now agrees that it is a work of art of the first importance. That is not to say that its admirers do not find problems in it. There is, for example, the variety of themes, which amount almost to a congestion. How did Plato succeed in bringing all his themes into artistic coherence? (vii)

So troubled by the complex form of the *Phaedrus* that they perceive it as a mess—congestion—these critics distill unity from the admitted complexity by applying the terms of managerial criticism:

Plato appears to employ two chief means to effect unity. The first of these is structure. It is dialectic, the highest form of discourse, that Plato uses to organize into a concrete unity the apparently incongruous topics of love and rhetoric. . . . The second means is style: the literary devices contribute to establishing the prevailing tone, which is that of light irony . . . [and create] a unity of mood suitable to the unity of situation. (vii–viii)

Such an assessment comprehends the *Phaedrus* by setting it in the intellectual "concrete" that hardens the "apparently incongruous" form of the dialogue into a mold of complementary unities. Thus stabilized, the *Phaedrus* becomes "an example of right discourse as well as an exposition of its principles" (viii). As a unified exposition of discourse principles, the *Phaedrus* is more a "lesson" than a drama, and the rhetoric Plato enfranchises becomes identified with rules and ingredients, such as those summarized by Everett Lee Hunt in his well-known essay, "Plato and Aristotle on Rhetoric and Rhetoricians":

1. "The first rule of good speaking is that the mind of the speaker should know the truth of what he is going to say." This cannot be interpreted as an injunction to speak the truth at all times. It is rather to *know* the truth in order (a) to be persuasive by presenting to the audience something which at least resembles truth, and (b) to avoid being oneself deceived by probabilities. In order to know the truth, the rhetorician must be a philosopher.
2. The rhetorician must define his terms, and see clearly what subjects are debatable and what are not. He must also be able to classify particulars under a general head, or to break up universals into particulars. The rhetorician, then, must be a logician.
3. Principles of order and arrangement must be introduced. "Every discourse ought to be a living creature, having its own body and head and feet; there ought to be a middle, beginning, and end, which are in a manner agreeable to one another and to the whole."

4. The nature of the soul must be shown, and after having "arranged men and speeches, and their modes and affections in different classes, and fitted them into one another, he will point out the connection between them—he will show why one is naturally persuaded by a particular form of argument, and another not." In other words, the rhetorician must be a psychologist.

5. The rhetorician must "speak of the instruments by which the soul acts or is affected in any way." Here we have the division under which comes practically all of rhetoric when viewed more narrowly and technically. The "instruments" by which rhetoric affects the soul are style and delivery. Plato believed style to be acquired, however, as Pericles acquired it, by "much discussion and lofty contemplation of nature."

6. The art of writing will not be highly regarded; nor will continuous and uninterrupted discourse be regarded as equal to cross-examination as a means of instruction. This is Plato's way of saying that any method of attempting to persuade multitudes must suffer from the very fact that it is a multitude which is addressed, and that the best of rhetoric is unequal to philosophic discussion.

7. The rhetorician will have such a high moral purpose in all his work that he will ever be chiefly concerned about saying that which is "acceptable to God." Rhetoric, then, is not an instrument for the determination of scientific truth, nor for mere persuasion regardless of the cause; it is an instrument for making the will of God prevail. The perfect rhetorician, as a philosopher, knows the will of God. (Howes 49–50)[4]

The activity of philosophical rhetoric, as revealed by Plato, taunts what Hunt represents: the managerial reduction of discourse to summary and the pedagogical extension of that tendency. Understanding the *Phaedrus* as a unified system of discourse principles, or as a lesson about love or wisdom or beauty, we mimic the limitations of Phaedrus himself, the boy who would rather acquire and memorize facts and concepts than ask questions. At the outset, Phaedrus wants to demonstrate that he "knows" Lysias's speech on love with a summary:

As far as the main points are concerned—practically every-thing Lysias said about the differences between the lover and the non-lover—I can summarize for you, topic by topic, beginning right at the start. (228)[5]

Phaedrus—much like the modern student absorbed with copying rather than questioning the stuff of lectures—identifies learning and knowing with information, or "points" (thus Phaedrus, intent upon rehearsing the speech, has asked Lysias to deliver it twice).

For Phaedrus, the "outstanding quality of the speech" is its completeness: "of all the points of the subject worthy to be enu-merated [Lysias] has neglected not one." His appreciation is bounded by the conventions of his education, by the rhetorical "common-places" or lines of argument with which he is familiar, as Socrates maintains:

Who do you suppose, in stating that one ought to comply with a non-lover rather than a lover, could omit to praise the prudence of one and to blame the folly of the other? These are, of course, commonplaces; what else could one say? (236)

The scope of Lysias's arguments coincides with the scope of Phae-drus's critical capacity; hence the student's insistence that he has heard a correct and comprehensive discussion of love. He likes what he hears because he hears what he "knows"; the question "what else could one say?" never occurs to Phaedrus.

Determined to merely reify and repeat the speech of Lysias, Phaedrus is an extreme example of critical blindness to ambiguity. As Ronna Burger concludes, "Phaedrus's interest in Lysias's speech is absorbed by his desire to memorize it; Socrates' interest in the speech is stimulated by the perplexities raised in thinking through its inexplicit assumptions" (13). Socrates wants to ask questions. From the beginning of the *Phaedrus*, the Phaedric conception of discourse as a source of unambiguous information, as reducible to determinant facts and principles, meets the Socratic question, "What else could one say?"

For Socrates, discourse—in this case a written speech—is an opportunity for philosophy, for questions that enlarge the arena of inquiry. By discouraging the attempt of Phaedrus to summarily report what the speech of Lysias is "about," Plato begins his evasion of a Phaedric version of his dialogue.

Warned against a Phaedric reduction of the *Phaedrus*, we are nonetheless faced with pronouncements by Socrates that *invite* reiteration as principles. Consider, for instance, Socrates' statement of the conditions for a "true art of rhetoric," delivered at the request of his rather dull-witted student:

Socrates: Now I think we have pretty well cleared up the question of what is and what is not art.

Phaedrus: Yes, I did think so; but just remind me again how we did it.

S: A man must first know the truth about every single subject on which he speaks or writes. He must be able to define each in terms of a universal class that stands by itself. When he has successively defined his subjects according to their specific classes, he must know how to continue the division until he reaches the point of indivisibility. He must make the same sort of distinction with reference to the nature of the soul. He must then discover the kind of speech that matches each type of nature. When that is accomplished, he must arrange and adorn each speech in such a way as to present complicated and unstable souls with complex speeches, speeches exactly attuned to every changing mood of the complicated soul—while the simple soul must be presented with simple speech. Not until a man acquires this capacity will it be possible to produce speech in a scientific way, in so far as its nature permits such treatment, either for the purposes of instruction or of persuasion. This is what our entire past discussion has brought to light.

P: Yes, that was certainly what we came to see. (277)

Socrates' speech here, especially the first sentence, is often the source of Platonic precepts on the art of rhetoric (see Hunt above). However, the dramatic context of these pronouncements renders the passage highly ironic, even self-contradictory. Socrates is delivering a pithy summary for Phaedrus, who is once again anxious to commit to memory the primary points of his teacher. The boy's request for summation indicates his trouble following Socrates, and his empty responses, here and elsewhere, comprise a litany of acquiescence: "It is indeed . . . Quite so . . . Surely . . . Yes . . . Quite right . . . You're quite right about that, too." Thus, while we cannot altogether dismiss Socrates' words here as unimportant, we should realize that this "packaged" information is a vehicle for ridiculing, or at least teasing, Phaedrus, and by extension, teasing Phaedric readers anxious to extract precepts.

Further, the procedure summarized by Socrates in step-by-step fashion, and accepted by Phaedrus as if it were plain and simple, is impossible. The presentation of "speeches exactly attuned to every changing mood of the complicated soul" cannot be mistaken as a practical injunction by any who recognize the compass of Socrates' requirements.[6] In sum, while Plato is emphasizing that a rhetor must know the truth, he is exploiting the confusion of philosophic truth—gained through *participation* in discourse—with its separation from the life of intellectual exchange in the form of principles and summaries; and he is admitting the disjunction between philosophical rhetoric—which investigates the suppleness of truth—and the practical matter of making speeches. Briefly put, Socrates' conclusions are hardly conclusive.

The elements of discourse conventionally associated with the *Phaedrus*, stressing the importance of classification, order, and arrangement, are mentioned in the same summary at issue here; as philosophical and rhetorical terms these elements partake of the same ambiguity that we have been noting. When Socrates associates classification, order, and arrangement with a conception of discourse as a living creature (264), he admits infinite variegation associated with "every changing mood of the complicated soul." The *Phaedrus* calls into question stable elements of discourse with the scope of such generalizations as this one, and with the discontinuity and playfulness that inform the dialogue throughout. It is a medley, of definitions of love and rhetoric, of myths and metaphors, of multiple Socratic "identities" (lover, madman, orator, philosopher); a medley whose beauty is, as Jowett proposes, a *tour de force*, attributable to the scope of its intellectual play.

The most obvious irresolution in the *Phaedrus*—between oral discourse and writing—is most easily resolved by extracting Socrates' explicit disparagements of writing to conclude, as Hunt does

above, that "the art of writing will not be highly regarded" in
Plato's philosophy.[7] Of course, such a conclusion compromises the
fact that the *Phaedrus* is written, and that Plato, in contradistinction
to his mistrust of written philosophy in the (possibly spurious)
Seventh Letter, was a prolific writer. Further, this dialogue between
Socrates and Phaedrus, which concludes with the summary dis-
missal of writing as a true art, is generated *by* writing, by the
speech of Lysias. The most accessible summary distinction between
oral discourse and writing is delivered by Phaedrus, not Socrates,
in a rare departure from the empty affirmations and bafflement that
typify the boy's responses. Phaedrus distorts the metaphysics of
Socrates' definition of discourse "inscribed with genuine knowledge
in the soul of the learner" (Burger 99) into a simpler, general
distinction between speaking and writing, between "living, animate
discourse" and the "ghost of it":

> S: Well then, are we able to imagine another sort of discourse,
>   a legitimate brother of our bastard? How does it originate?
>   How far is it better and more powerful in nature?
> P: What sort of discourse? What do you mean about its origin?
> S: A discourse which is inscribed with genuine knowledge in
>   the soul of the learner; a discourse that can defend itself and
>   knows to whom it should speak and before whom to keep
>   silent.
> P: Do you mean the living, animate discourse of a man who
>   really knows? Would it be fair to call the written discourse
>   only a kind of ghost of it?
> S: Precisely. (276)

With his recognition that Phaedrus's distinction is precise, Socrates
proceeds to ambiguate it, with an analogy to a farmer sowing seeds
that praises the discourse of the dialectician "sowing words" in a
congenial soul, an analogy that trivializes writing done "for the
mere fun of it," but maintains the serious importance of dialectical
writing (Burger 100), the deliberate generation of "words which
will not be unproductive," which will cause the "growth of fresh
words" in "other natures" (276).

When Plato complicates and extends Phaedrus's separation
of speaking and writing, he makes suspect both the boy's simple-

minded distinction and like distinctions that may arise from the urgency to extract accessible precepts. Presuming, as we read Socrates' disparagement of writing, that Plato means what Socrates says (an undecidable issue), we see that the philosopher mistrusts, in particular, writing that provokes (or means to provoke) certainty or clarity:

P: What did we say?
S: That, whether Lysias or anyone else who has ever or will ever lay down laws in written form, either in private or in public, and think that in composing a document for a political maneuver, he achieves thereby great certainty or clarity— this sort of composition is a disgrace to the writer, no matter whether one affirms or denies it. For ignorance, whether conscious or not, of justice and injustice, good and evil, cannot possibly fail to involve reproach of the most shameful sort, even though the whole mob applauds it.
P: Quite so.
S: On the other hand, there is the man who thinks that the written word on any subject necessarily contains much that is playful, and that no work, whether in verse or prose, has ever been written or recited that is worthy of serious attention—and this applies to the recitations of rhapsodes also, delivered for the sake of mere persuasion, which give no opportunity for questioning or exposition—the truth is that the best of these works merely serves to remind us of what we know already. (277–78)

The writer who attempts to induce certainty or clarity is distinguished from the man who acknowledges the dangerous "playfulness" of writing, playfulness which invites rather than silences the questioning of the philosopher. Seduced by the promise of hearing what Lysias has written, Socrates had countered Phaedrus's all-too-ready assent with his probe of the ambiguity of the speech. Thus he set in motion the philosophic discourse that plays with language in order to transcend it, to approach the ideal eternal memory written in the soul (276).

Given the condemnation of clarity and certainty in writing, both in the words of Socrates and in the variegated form of the dialogue, we should be less disposed to regard the *Phaedrus* as a tissue of information than as a collection of prompts to further discourse, as the interplay of ambiguities, the stuff of philosophy. Ronna Burger, whose stimulating scholarship has informed parts of this discussion so far, reaches this conclusion in *Plato's* Phaedrus: *A Defense of the Philosophical Art of Writing:* "Only when the potential ambiguity of the product of writing is acknowledged, thus obliterating trust in its clarity and firmness, does it have the power to set in motion the internal process of thought" (77); she proposes further that Platonic writing is "precisely that written work which betrays an awareness of its own lack of clarity and firmness . . ." (91).

Writing depends upon the concealment of ambiguity for its persuasive power. Plato is calling into question the seemingly "neutral" discourse represented by Lysias's speech: wholly conventional and acceptable, but not at all provocative (Weaver 9). This is the sort of writing that Thamus rejects (*Phaedrus* 275) as inculcating in students "the delusion that they have wide knowledge; while they are, in fact, for the most part incapable of real judgment." Recall that Phaedrus pretends to have acquired such knowledge by studying Lysias's speech (235); he does not recognize himself as the sort of student to whom Thamus refers and initially dismisses Socrates' story of Thamus and Theuth as fanciful: "Now Socrates, it's perfectly easy for you to make up tales from Egypt or anywhere else you please" (275). The Phaedrus who had readily accepted the more plain and prosaic writing of Lysias, writing which Socrates reveals as fraudulent, suspects as manipulative the more "literary" discourse of Socrates, a text whose ambiguity—rooted in uncertain origins and the revisions that may have occurred over time— Socrates readily admits: "Whether it's true or not, only [our ancestors] know" (274). For Plato, writing which pretends to be clear, factual, and final in its pronouncements—*plain* writing—lies.

The writing in the *Phaedrus* reveals rather than conceals ambiguity and exploits incompleteness and play. The play of evasion and coercion introduces Socrates' first speech:

S: But, dear Phaedrus, I shall make myself ridiculous if I speak extempore, an amateur beside a trained professional, and on the same subject!

P: Listen to me and stop your foolishness. I'm nearly certain that *I* can say something to compel you to speak.

S: Then please don't say it!

P: That's precisely what I intend to do. It's an oath. "I swear to you by" . . . but by whom? by what god? Perhaps this plane tree? "I swear to you by this plane tree that if you don't speak your speech in its presence, I shall never, never, never recite you a speech by any author whatsoever—never even let you have work of another!"

S: Woe! Alas! Wretch! How well you've discovered how to compel a lover of words to carry out your commands. (236)

Socrates, the fool/tease/teacher/lover of boys-words-truth here allows/resists/invites/succumbs to the compulsion/naiveté/coquetry/violence of this student/lover/"other"/wretch. As the dialogue continues, possibilities for naming what the characters are "about" increase as the context of the discussion expands. Socrates' second speech, with its famous myth of the charioteer, improves upon the earlier speeches with its comprehensiveness; it includes the eternal past, reaches beyond the heavens, and with an erotic description of the soul's desire (251), embraces the grossly physical, the mythic, and the divine at once. Incongruous realms and identities comprise the "grammar" of Plato's writing, which tends to multiply rather than conceal the varieties of meaning.

Lysias's pretentious and narrow speech is removed from philosophy and philosophical writing because it is a partial view, as Phaedrus seems to sense when he declares initially that "the topic [of Lysias's speech] was, *in a way*, love" (227, my emphasis).[8] Socrates' trivialization of the speech through progressive expansion of the concept of love defines the activity of philosophy as persistent and multifarious attempts to recollect the "content of a general term" (the *ostensible* term, in this case, is love). The intellectual capacity for probing the ambiguity of language—for it is language that signifies "what we now assert to be real"—distinguishes human life:

For to be a man one must understand the content of a general term, leaving the field of manifold sense perceptions, and entering that in which the object of knowledge is unique and

grasped only by reasoning. This process is a remembering of
what our soul once saw as it made its journey with a god,
looking down upon what we now assert to be real and gazing
upwards at what is Reality itself. . . . And if a man makes a
right use of such entities as memoranda, always being perfectly initiated into perfect mysteries, he alone becomes truly
perfected. He separates himself from the busy interests of
men and approaches the divine. He is rebuked by the vulgar
as insane, for they cannot know that he is possessed by
divinity. (249)

Here memory is associated with a dialectical process of shifting
gazes, by the philosopher who considers the expansiveness of "what
we now assert to be real" *in terms of* "Reality itself." Moving closer
to Reality is consistent with a broader view of "the field of manifold
sense perceptions," which one enlarges through "a right use of
such entities as memoranda."

The "right" use of writing, as a reminder "of what we know
already" (278) means enlarging the field of inquiry, which is what
this passage and the entire dialogue are "about." Faced with placing
the *Phaedrus* in intellectual history, and moved by its statements
on rhetoric and writing to form particular conclusions on those
issues, we find ourselves wondering what the dialogue is about,
only to realize, once we abandon the extraction of lessons and
principles, that "about" may be reconsidered not as a preposition
restricting an object, but as a verb, as a synonym for doing or
making as in "out and about." In this sense, the *Phaedrus* is about
the art of wondering, about rhetoric and writing and reading as
play with an expanding horizon.

Aristotle, *The "Art" of Rhetoric*

It is common to equate a knowledge of the *Rhetoric* with
information "in" the *Rhetoric*. Thus Aristotle's text is regarded as
a body of precepts and principles that can be represented sche-
matically. Any such summary reduction must begin with devas-
tating assumptions about philosophical writing in general and Aristotle
in particular: 1) knowledge/philosophy is a definite unity of prop-

ositions, to be contained and consumed; 2) Aristotle would agree.
Finding that the *Rhetoric* is rife with inconsistency, meandering,
and sketchiness, prosaic admirers who associate the greatness of
philosophy and philosophers with clarity, control, and coherent
"substance" may have to conclude, along with J. H. Randall, that
the muddled *Rhetoric* is corrupt:

> The Aristotelian documents are fragmentary, and frequently
> break off; they are repetitious, and often display little clear
> order in their parts. Still more, they exhibit manifest con-
> tradictions, of approach, of mood, of theory, even of fun-
> damental position and "doctrine." The obvious reason for
> this somewhat chaotic character is that our present text is
> not as Aristotle left it. (23)

Other scholars agree with Randall, speculating that inconsistencies
in the text may reflect a "too many cooks" phenomenon, the result
of a number of Aristotle's followers each taking a hand in revising
the original. Others contend that Aristotle himself consistently
revised the *Rhetoric*, perhaps over twenty years, so that what we
read now is not the result of multiple intrusions by Aristotelians,
but of multiple reconsiderations by a rhetor seeing his subject
anew: "He arrived at his precepts by a long and tortuous pathway;
he advanced to a new position only to fall back and take up another
position later" (Hill 192). The question of how the *Rhetoric* we
have in hand was composed remains unresolved. (The irresolute
history of the composition of the *Rhetoric* is summarized by David
Blakesley in his unpublished thesis on "Manner as Form in Aristotle's *Rhetoric*.") The long persistence of that question points up
the historical disaffiliation of Aristotle with philosophical license;
as Ingram Bywater proposes:

> Doubts and suspicions start from a certain preconceived idea,
> inherited from the Middle Ages, of the general character of
> the Aristotelian writings—that the "master of them that
> know" could never for a moment forget his logic; that his
> mind worked with all the sureness of a machine; and that a
> treatise of his must not only have been written throughout
> on the straightest lines, but also have left his hands as free

from oversights and inconsistencies as a modern published work is expected to be. The untenableness of these assumptions, as thus stated, is obvious. . . . Aristotle, with all his scientific formalism, is even as a thinker much more human than we are apt to suppose. (xiii)

Reading within the traditions of genre and reputation associated with the *Rhetoric*, one expects not only to share the author's *mastery* of the subject, but also to follow his *intellectual progress* toward a comprehensive description of the art of rhetoric. One thus expects a sequence of parts marked by an increase in information and certainty: the farther we read, the more we (and Aristotle) will know. Such an expectation is reinforced at several points in the text, when Aristotle makes pronouncements of seeming finality. Consider, for example, the closing words of the *Rhetoric*, which exemplify a fitting peroration while they also punctuate the whole work: " 'I have done; you all have heard; you have the facts; give your judgement' " (1420b; the Cooper translation is cited throughout). The finality of this statement is an orator's trick; it promises that the auditors "have the facts" and are therefore advised to stop deliberation for the sake of judgment. Of course, they don't have the facts at all, in any neutral or comprehensive sense, but rather the "things that gain our belief" (1378a), the orator's carefully biased appeal to assent.

As the auditors of the *Rhetoric*, we are advised through this final statement that the facts of the matter—rhetoric—have been given, and that the subject is closed. However, given the rather obvious fraudulence of the peroration as such—especially in light of Aristotle's ongoing disclosure through the *Rhetoric* that all facts and judgments are permutations, not absolutes—we should not accept the advice to pronounce the *Rhetoric* "finished," nor can we be sure that Aristotle wants us to do so. If we consider even briefly the questions of intention and meaning provoked by Aristotle's peroration, it becomes an *opening* statement rather than a closing one, a statement on the impossibility of clearly conjoining information and judgment, a disclosure of the tangle of interpretive possibilities that fill the activity of rhetoric. Nothing plain here.

Taken "literally," the closing statement of the *Rhetoric* is an example of the appropriate style for a peroration; it is an asyndeton, or statement without conjunctions. Taken thus, the closing is rather inconsequential, the reiteration of conventional grammar. It may be dismissed as something of an afterthought, perhaps, a fragmentary and brief rush to finish up the arrangement section. Yet this peroration does follow up, for a moment, Aristotle's extended commentary on asyndeton in the middle of Book III (1413b), where he stresses the "dramatic effect" of such a construction; specifically, the special ability of asyndeta for "making it seem that a number of statements have been made in the time required for one." One function of asyndeton, then, is to create an impression of comprehensiveness and magnitude; the very brevity of each general proposition (e.g., "you have the facts") entails a sweep of impressions—held by the auditors—that amplify it. Closing thus, Aristotle recalls and emphasizes the range of his *Rhetoric*; however, against this peroration stands his earlier discussion of asyndeton, as a warning to those affected by syntactic trickery. In sum, the peroration may be taken as a brief stylistic example, a conventional reminder, a hurried tag, an extension of earlier discussion, an appreciation of the comprehensiveness of the *Rhetoric*, a warning to those easily impressed by asyndeta, an echo of Lysias's conclusion to "Against Erotosthenes" (as J. H. Freese has proposed), and—insofar as the peroration points back generally to the "facts" of the *Rhetoric* and specifically to the treatment of asyndeton—as an index to what has been written.

Further, the peroration is an index to other statements in the *Rhetoric* that are alike in kind, statements featured by Aristotle as complete, final, the "last word." The peroration, as a conclusion, is hardly conclusive, and calls into question the summary reiteration of any of Aristotle's assured pronouncements as stable principles or straight information on rhetoric.

Investigating what Aristotle means by rhetoric, we conclude that the principles of discourse are supple, inclusive, and finally indeterminate. For Aristotle, rhetoric functions "to find out in each case the existing means of persuasion" (1355b). The art of rhetoric is an art of invention, of hypothesizing different variables informing a speech situation, and reflecting on how the situation is affected. The beliefs and presuppositions of the auditors, the character of the rhetor, the context and occasions for the speech, the prevailing conventions of language: these characteristics are always in flux, and

Aristotle demonstrates the array of questions that a rhetor must consistently pose to himself in order to invent possibilities for creating meaning, community, and goodwill. A rhetor's exploration is propelled by indeterminacy; the uncertainty of any speech situation makes truth a matter of probability.

Rhetoric is an art because, first of all, the rhetorical invention of perspectives can be pursued methodically; for Aristotle, the inventory of variables constitutes a systematic, thus artistic, investigation. Add to this idea of art another, quite appropriate one, from Aristotle's *Nichomachean Ethics*. There art is "the coming into being of something which is capable of being different from what it is."[9] This definition both complements and complicates the investigative system offered in the *Rhetoric*. The art of rhetoric underlines the ambiguity of language; to practice the art, one remains mindful that all conclusions are provisional, tentative. The art lies not in the completion of a text, but in the transfiguration of one text—one system of possibilities—into another.

Early in Book I, Aristotle warns that understanding the art of rhetoric must not be confused with accruing information: "to enumerate and classify the usual subjects of public business and deliberation" is appropriate to a more exact and narrow subject than rhetoric. Rhetoric has little to do with the survey of established categories; rather, it is an activity at once logical, political, philosophical, and psychological: it "combines the science of logical analysis with the ethical branch of political science, and is akin partly to dialectic, partly to sophistical argument" (1359b). One immobilizes rhetoric by converting it from a habit of mind to a body of data, discouraging the collocation of perspectives which define the "nature" of rhetoric, perspectives which—taken together—reveal the ambiguity and maintain the uncertainty which create more rhetoric.

After declaring that "to enumerate and classify the usual subjects of public business and deliberation" is unsuited to rhetoric, Aristotle turns at once to these very subjects, albeit without intending "exhaustive scrutiny," proposing that

> Of the subjects upon which all men deliberate and upon which deliberative orators speak, the chief ones, we may say, are five in number, to wit: 1) ways and means; and 2) war

and peace; next, 3) national defense; and 4) imports and exports; finally, 5) legislation.

To this point, in the space of scarcely a page, Aristotle has warned against confusing the activity of rhetoric with the explication of subjects; contradicted his own warning; and limited the arena of deliberation to five subjects which seem neither equivalent in scope nor categorically distinctive, five subjects whose exclusive importance as the foundations of deliberation is, at least, arguable.

In the passage above, Aristotle's peremptory tone, conditioned by his enumerative specificity, helps to create an impression of the *Rhetoric* as intentionally assured, conclusive, and complete and to align these qualities with the activity of rhetoric itself. However, such an impression is unsettled by both the indefinite character of the terms he enumerates and by the meandering discussion surrounding this passage. Negotiating the turns that Aristotle has taken in this brief space, turns which point up the ambiguity and even arbitrariness of his own intellection here, we experience the rhetor "doing" rhetoric, collapsing content and method, setting aside analytical precision while he sketches lines of thought that enter and proceed from one another with the abruptness congenial to a licentious mind, and an unconnectedness only scarcely concealed by cursory transitions ("nevertheless" is the singular bridge from Aristotle's disparagement of enumerating subjects to his engagement in just that, in both the Cooper and Freese translations).

As a cue to the essentially sketchy and speculative nature of the enumeration above, the phrase "we may say" (translated thus by both Cooper and Freese) asks us to recognize the tentativeness of the five chosen subjects; an alternate set, we suppose, might be proposed. Aristotle is not offering core categories here, but rather, opportunities for demonstrating that even when rhetoric is engaged with "subjects," it cannot be reduced to a closed set of facts. Quite the contrary: Aristotle's *Rhetoric* proposes that facts are inexhaustible. As William Grimaldi remarks in his commentary on the *Rhetoric* (which invites further discussion below), "No subject is fully exhausted until intelligent queries can no longer be raised" (117). As Aristotle demonstrates with his sketch of the large, interrelated *loci* for inquiries about ways and means, war and peace, etc., the rhetor's deliberation proceeds from issues that are, of themselves, not determinate; he may wander rather abruptly outside the subject proper and must always stop at a point that is arbitrary rather than really final. Aristotle's remarks on legislation, with their casual brevity and ragged procession, are scarcely useful as a guide to areas for study, suggestive instead of the importance of a mind following its own lead:

> For the stability of the commonwealth, the deliberative speaker . . . must be competent in legislation, for the salvation of the State is in its laws. Accordingly, one must know how many types of government there are; what conditions are favorable to each type; and what things, inherent in the type itself, or antagonistic to it from without, naturally tend to destroy it. When I speak of destruction by causes inherent in the type itself, I mean that, save for the best type, they are all ruined by getting unstrung and by over-tension. Thus democracy grows weaker, not only by relaxation, until it ends in oligarchy, but also by excessive tension; just as the acquiline or snub nose, as its curve is relaxed, comes toward the intermediate type, but when the hook or the snub is violently intensified, it assumes a shape as to lose all resemblance to a nose.
>
> For the ends of legislation, it is helpful to understand what type of government is desirable, and to learn this not only from the history of our own State, but also by studying the forms of government abroad, observing how the different forms are suited to different peoples. And hence, obviously, books of travel will be of use with respect to legislation, since from them one may learn the laws and customs of foreign nations; while histories should be read for their bearing upon councils of state. All these inquiries, however, belong to Political Science, not to Rhetoric. (1360a)

Following a daunting injunction to develop the calculus of relationships among types of governments, favorable conditions, and causes of destruction, and thus to envelop oneself in matters that are always fluctuating (now, for the modern rhetor, more than ever), Aristotle selects a presumably puzzling set—destructive "causes inherent in the type itself"——for further explication. Rather than explaining with political "data," he resorts to fanciful, rather far-fetched, disjunctive and funny analogies to stringed instruments and noses. This is the rhetor enlarging the scope of his subject rather baldly, beyond Political Science proper, in order to allow and exploit the intellectual play that at once vivifies and departs from the concept under discussion, moving back and forth between literal and figurative matters of fact, exploiting rhetoric as the discovery and synthesis of multiple perspectives.

Recovering from literary fancy, Aristotle virtually repeats what he has already emphasized, that "it is helpful to understand what type of government is desirable"; the recursion to this "central" point allows him to widen the circumference of inquiry still further, by elaborating the geographic scope of the rhetor's concerns to include "forms of government abroad." Aristotle forces an arbitrary end to this elaboration, having earlier excused himself from "exhaustive scrutiny," with the further excuse that this sketch of the "chief subjects upon which the intending deliberative speaker should be well-informed" (1360b) is inviting the specification that belongs to Political Science proper. Thus Aristotle distinguishes the activity of generating inquiries—which is Rhetoric—from a body of data which is subject to such inquiry.

Further, and more important for this study, Aristotle here distinguishes the form of rhetorical inquiry from the enumeration of predetermined subjects, by exploiting analogy, recursion, elaboration, and forced closure as movements of mind that impose no particular pattern upon inquiry, while they also constitute types of intellection and ways of understanding that become available only in the course of speculation. The activity of rhetoric is not the filling in of discursive forms; it is, rather, the formation of forms, via shifting among categories of understanding with a persistent whimsy, in order to create a temporary scaffold for constructions of even greater complexity.

For Aristotle, the rhetor's "progress" as he explores does not entail greater clarity and precision; this is especially the case for Aristotle himself. At the beginning of Book II, where he seems initially to sum up and move ahead, Aristotle is caught up quickly in a recursive tangle. To begin a discussion of ethical proofs, he first stresses the end, or object of rhetoric, which is judgment, and immediately ambiguates the concept of judgment by assessing its complications:

> Now Rhetoric finds its end in judgment—for the audience judges the counsels that are given, and the decision is a judgment; and hence the speaker must not merely see to it that his speech shall be convincing and persuasive, but he must give the right impression of himself, and get his judge into the right state of mind. . . . To the friendly judge, the person about whom he is making a decision will seem either quite innocent or guilty of no great wrong; to the inimical judge, the same person will seem just the opposite. To the man that is eager and hopeful, the proposed object, if pleasant, seems a thing that will come to pass and will be good; to the man that is apathetic or disgruntled, the same object seems just the opposite. (1378a)

The very instability of judges (here a term large enough to include modern judges of discourse, namely, critical readers) renders judgment a matter that can be explored but not ensured. By focusing on the *end* of rhetoric, one initiates another open-ended inquiry, whose extent becomes more apparent as Aristotle continues with an enumeration of the elements of ethical proof:

> . . . there are three things that gain our belief, namely, intelligence, character, and good will. Speakers are untrustworthy in what they say or advise from one or more of the following causes. Either through want of intelligence they form wrong opinions; or, while they form correct opinions, their rascality leads them to say what they do not think; or, while intelligent and honest enough, they are not well disposed, and so perchance will fail to advise the best course, though they see it. This is a complete list of the possibilities.

Evincing the lack of system that informs his discussion, as well as the interactive range of the terms he presents, Aristotle refers to his discussion of virtues in Book I for further "information" on intelligence and good character, and promises that he will discuss "good will and a friendly disposition" later in Book

II. Thus, pointing forward in his text to further discussion of one
of the elements of ethical proof (1381a–1382a) and backward to
a scuttled discussion of other elements (1366a), Aristotle is once
again sorting and distributing the terms that arise while he delib-
erates, reinforcing the sense that no linear procedure suffices when
one is thinking things through.

The main problem for rhetoric, criticism, and philosophy—
activities intent upon "things that gain our belief," provided here
with a "complete list of the possibilities"—is the ambiguity of the
possibilities themselves: intelligence, character, and good will, even
somewhat amplified as they are here, serve as conceptual *prompts*
to inquiry; the inquiry expands and contracts as the terms it
includes are reformulated, and emphases change. In this instance,
the *Rhetoric* has moved quickly from the introduction of the three
elements of ethical proof to the postponement or relocation of
their further consideration, to a departure from this at once assured
and brachiated introduction for a new introduction, to the emotions, en route to another look at good will:

> As for good will and a friendly disposition, these must be
> discussed under the head of the emotions. By these, the
> emotions, are meant those states which are attended by pain
> and pleasure, and which, as they change, make a difference
> in our judgments; for example: anger, pity, fear, and all the
> like, and also their opposites. With respect to each emotion
> the points to be determined are three.

Here good will, which is a master term of ethical proof, is "reduced" to a subcategory of emotion, just as intelligence and character were relegated to subcategories of virtue. In the space of a
few sentences, the conceptual "size" of the elements of ethical
proof has become ambiguous, so that it is difficult to tell, in the
midst of this *Rhetoric* which repeatedly implies a *schema* of inquiry
with its reliance on definitive enumeration, which are the super-
categories and which are the subcategories, and how the connecting
lines between them should be drawn.

Of course, if we read the *Rhetoric* as philosophical or practical
"information," we set aside the complications or attempt to unify

them somehow, so that some "yield" eventuates from the text. William Grimaldi's impressive effort to establish the unity of the *Rhetoric* and dismiss those critics who have denigrated Aristotle's inconsistencies is based on the assumption that a "unified" *Rhetoric* is *better*, more worthy of Aristotle, than a disunified one. Grimaldi acknowledges that "the logical coherence of the treatise, as it has come down to us . . . has been denied for a number of reasons: . . . textual inconsistencies, repetitions, contradictions, obscurity of statement, as well as the apparent failure of the author to follow out in detail programmatic statements which give the organization of the work"; at the same time Grimaldi repeatedly insists that "there is a highly developed coherence within the work" and goes on to explicate that coherence more fully than any other modern commentator (28ff.). Rather than take issue with Grimaldi's explication, I mean to suggest here that the presupposition which initiates his argument as well as the arguments of Aristotle's denigrators—that a consistent, coherent *Rhetoric* is "better" than a lively jumble—is where a reconsideration of the *Rhetoric* and of philosophical writing must start. Paolo Valesio suggests such a reconsideration, as part of his argument against "colonizing" rhetoric in *Novantiqua*, proposing that Aristotle's *Rhetoric* evinces a "groping attitude . . . a tendency to strike out into many different paths, trying them out for a brief time" (25).

At best, in the hands of scholars such as Grimaldi, the urgency to reify the *Rhetoric* as a coherent system is an illuminating demonstration of how one might grapple with an elusive text, a demonstration of the relentless human disposition toward wholeness. At worst, in the hands of those who would "use" the *Rhetoric* as a prescriptive authority, the reduction of Aristotle's excursion to a relatively stable "system" makes it irrelevant to modern and postmodern conceptions of philosophy, rhetoric, and literacy. A recent assessment of Aristotle's *Rhetoric*, in Philip Arrington's "Tropes of the Composing Process," represents the schematizing and scientizing of Aristotle which, as Arrington suggests by presenting his argument as noncontroversial, has been widely accepted.

Turning to Aristotle, who as a "scientist of discourse" is the forerunner of modern empiricists of composition, Arrington portrays the *Rhetoric* as a sharp departure from the Platonic model of discourse-as-drama. In line with the tradition that distinguishes Plato as the "philosopher" and Aristotle as the "technician," Arrington categorizes Aristotelian rhetoric under the aegis of metonymy: Aristotle "reduces a complex whole to its parts and names the whole in terms of laws that bind these parts." The transformation-via-reduction of the complexity of discourse to "a set of techniques" is Aristotle's metonymy:

> Thus, Aristotle simplifies the causes of eloquence into the discovery of the best means to a certain end. The end determines those means just as it determines the type of discourse composed. The ends themselves he defines in terms of time—past, present, or future; and the composing process he outlines consists of at least two steps, finding something to say and saying it. To complete the first step, the orator must discover those *topoi* which apply to the issue in question. . . . Once they're found, the orator arranges them, stating his arguments and then his proof, and expressing both in an ordinary, clear, appropriate, occasionally ornate style so that the arguments are more lively and vivid.
>
> Such, in the briefest form, is Aristotle's composing process. His description is linear, temporal, and causal. (328–29)

As a reductive metonymy, the *Rhetoric* enfranchises the compartmentalization of discourse and the linear sequencing of "steps" that lead through process to product. But Aristotle's *Rhetoric* is rather like Plato's *Phaedrus*, a "dramatistic" tissue of open philosophical inquiry that, of itself, represents the activity of rhetoric. Quite contrary to a reductive view of discourse, Aristotle demonstrates the impossibility of reduction. As I have argued with representative passages, Aristotle tends to ambiguate the content of his most decisive pronouncements, pronouncements neatly schematized by those who savor utilitarian rhetoric. Lurching about here and there, Aristotle does not present a weak or flawed rhetorical theory; one might say, rather, that he presents a *true* one, an unpretentious one, a theory that welcomes the instability (with its attendant problems) of thought and language.

Cicero, *De Oratore*

I might summarize my understanding of Plato's and Aristotle's rhetorical theories by declaring that Plato was not a Platonist and Aristotle was not an Aristotelian. The tradition of appreciation and interpretation that followed both figures from Antiquity has reified their works into lists of rules and principles that are respectively associated with "Platonic" or "Aristotelian" rhetoric, but dissociated from an art of wondering. Further, I propose that Cicero —perhaps the most influential name from ancient rhetorical theory—was not a Ciceronian. However, in separating Cicero from the Ciceronianism that flourished through the Middle Ages and beyond, I would not deny his advocacy of the static rules and principles that presume his influence. Cicero is one of the writers who contributes directly to a formulaic Roman rhetoric, which has been criticized recently because it promotes "a ceremonial view of discourse among students" and reduces writing to "a ritual performance" (Knoblauch and Brannon 31).

The Ciceronianism that Knoblauch and Brannon criticize, still strong in its application to competency in writing and rhetoric, is founded on works by Cicero that are ancillary to *De Oratore*. As James Murphy has pointed out, "Cicero's theories were known to the Middle Ages primarily through the highly schematized rhetorical treatises of his youthful period" (*Rhetoric in the Middle Ages* 109). *De Oratore* was known only in mutilated versions through the fifteenth century. George Kennedy adds that the *Ad Herrenium*, a pseudo-Ciceronian handbook that was attributed to Cicero well into the Middle Ages; and the *De Inventione*, Cicero's early attempt to reiterate the Standard Roman rules and principles of rhetoric that he had been taught, comprise the "standard theory of classical rhetoric" to which Cicero scarcely added anything new: "This standard theory of classical rhetoric, as taught from around 150 B.C. to the end of antiquity, is set forth systematically in a number of modern handbooks of the subject. . . . Some modern critics call it Ciceronian rhetoric. . . . [but] because he made only small personal contributions to the theory it is better to call it technical, or prescriptive, or standard classical rhetoric" (Kennedy, *Art* 89–90). When I propose that Cicero was not a Ciceronian, then, I mean to set apart his most original and radical consideration of rhetoric, and dissociate the "lost" Cicero from the Cicero who influenced, for instance, Thomas Wilson's *Arte of Rhetorique*, the sixteenth-century English handbook on rhetoric which served as a prototype for centuries following. Wilson's pronounced Ciceronianism "is most heavily indebted to *Ad Herrenium*, which until the time of Erasmus was thought to be Cicero" (Wagner 530).

However, Cicero's mature rhetorical theory, disclosed in all its complexity through the shifting dialogic viewpoints of *De Oratore* mitigates the importance of a recipe-rhetoric and represents the full intellectual play that Cicero purposefully restricts elsewhere. Positing *De Oratore* as the central Ciceronian text, Cicero's contribution to rhetoric can be understood, along with that of Plato and Aristotle, as the identification of rhetoric and writing with irresolution and ambiguity.

While we may dismiss *De Inventione* as scarcely representative of Cicero's mature conception of rhetoric, we should acknowledge and wonder about the *Partitiones Oratoriae* ("The Divisions of Oratory"), written soon after the *De Oratore*. In *Partitiones*, Cicero presents to his son a sketch of the conventional information about oratory represented by Hellenistic schooling, in the form of an exchange between Cicero "senior" and Cicero "junior," which H. Rackham has rightly called "the most purely scientific of all Cicero's writing on rhetoric" (306); a representative passage illustrates Rackham's assessment:

Cicero Junior: . . . So what have you to say about the rules that govern a speech?

Cicero Senior: That a speech consists of four divisions, of which the first and the last are the parts that serve for arousing emotion—introductions and perorations must appeal to the emotions—while the second division, narrative, and the third, proof, are the parts that procure belief in what is said. . . .

Cicero Junior: Proceed then and explain your four divisions to me *seriatim*.

Cicero Senior: I will, and I will start first from the introductory passages, which are derived either from the persons or from the facts of the case, and which are employed for three purposes: to secure for us a friendly hearing, an intelligent hearing, and an attentive hearing. (viii, 27)

Cicero senior admits that his instruction here consists mainly of "signposts" which may be preliminary to "much more important matters" (xl, 140). *Partitiones* presents the sort of schoolish information which, as we shall see, both Crassus and Antonius deride in *De Oratore*, the sort of systematic, coherent, conventional information preferred by the young and impatient students in the dialogue. The striking contrast between what Cicero provides his son and what he provides as a fully-expressed rhetorical theory reinforces Ralph Micken's speculation that the character of *Partitiones* reflects Cicero's attitude toward his son more than his conception of rhetoric; Micken concludes that "the broad philosophical approach of *De Oratore* would have been wasted on [Cicero's son]," who "seems to have shown none of the scholarly interest or aptitude of his father" (Micken xvii). Cicero's local and singular purpose in *Partitiones* results in a mechanistic handbook that recalls Cicero's own youthful and incomplete attempt to present a formulaic rhetoric, *De Inventione*, a work which he dismissed in *De Oratore* as "scarcely worthy of my present standing in life" (I, ii). Thus he contrasts a schoolish rhetorical theory, seemingly designed to placate dullards, with a mature conception of rhetoric that discourages the appetite for knowledge as information.

More than half of Cicero's final work on rhetoric, *Orator*, is a disquisition on sentence structure and rhythm. Here Cicero touts the elements of ornament in unprecedented detail; his obvious purpose is "a defense of his own oratorical practice" against the spare Attic style (Hubbell, in *Orator* 297). But still in this discussion, written nearly a decade after *De Oratore*, Cicero maintains the importance of the orator as philosopher, constantly engaged in speculation on all the subjects that affect human affairs:

For philosophy is essential to a full, copious and impressive discussion and exposition of the subjects which often come up in speeches and are usually treated meagerly, whether they concern religion, death, piety, patriotism, good and evil, virtues and vices, duty, pain, pleasure, or mental disturbances and errors. I am speaking now of the raw material of the speech, not about its literary style. (xxxiv, 118–19)

Further, while oratorical style is not the "raw material" that admits so broadly of philosophical speculation, the stylist must exercise a philosophical sensibility, an alertness to multiple meanings, because language is "soft, pliant, and so flexible that it follows wherever you turn it" (xvi, 52).

Attempting to distinguish between the "philosophical" Cicero and the "technical" Cicero, we find them both in the several works which profess rhetorical theory, so that Cicero's rhetoric emerges as a collection of contradictory and complementary perspectives: this advocate of conventional rules and academic prescriptions also dismisses them; this compiler of handbooks which represent rhetoric as a digest of standard advice claims that oratory is so complex and difficult an art that it can scarcely be mastered by anyone (De Oratore I, ii).

Concluding from a survey of his works that Cicero's views on rhetoric are diverse and irresolute, we are ready to consider that the inconsistences and different voices manifest in his corpus, taken together, signal that rhetoric for Cicero is defined by diversity, open speculation, and ambiguity. De Oratore exploits these qualities by dramatizing them; it is thus a more inclusive examination of rhetoric than any of Cicero's other works and represents most fully his identification of public discourse with a "vast number of things":

A knowledge of a vast number of things is necessary, without which volubility of words is empty and ridiculous; speech itself is to be formed, not merely by choice, but by careful construction of words; and all the emotions of the mind, which nature has given to man, must be intimately known; for all the force and art of speaking must be employed in allaying or exciting the feelings of those who listen. (I, v)

The real power of eloquence is such that it embraces the origin, the influence, the changes of all things in the world, all virtues, duties, and all nature, so far as it affects the manners, minds, and lives of mankind. (III, xx)

The first quotation comes from Cicero's introductory remarks preceding the dialogue; the second from one of Cicero's "characters," Lucius Crassus. Setting aside the question of whether Crassus speaks for Cicero, we can still note the similarity between their definitive statements on the art of eloquence: it is a global art, necessarily defined in global terms.[10] Students of the art must consider, in particular, "the whole of antiquity and a multitude of examples," "the knowledge of laws in general, or of the civil law in particular," as well as the "modulation and variation" of "look, voice, and gesture." Students are exhorted to "contemplate in their minds the full magnitude of the object" and not to trust that they can reach the height at which they aim by the aid of the (conventional, academic) "precepts, masters, and exercises" (I, v).

De Oratore is about the interplay of the vast number of things that Cicero sketches here. Just as Plato's *Phaedrus* and Aristotle's *Rhetoric* must not be mistaken as collections of information on rhetoric, but rather as specimens of the art of wondering, Cicero's dialogue must not be mistaken as an exposition. Rather, what we have here is a *demonstration* of the vast art sketched in the introduction, a demonstration which warns students against the tendency to reduce rhetoric to an academic box by dramatizing the impossibility of settling on the nature of eloquence and rhetorical effectiveness.

De Oratore presents a range of multiple perspectives across time which contribute to an ambiguous rhetorical theory. Cicero's Crassus summarizes standard advice when he insists that an orator must know history: "The writers and teachers in all the liberal arts must be read and turned over, and must, for the sake of exercise, be praised, interpreted, corrected, censured, refuted. . . . all antiquity must be known" (I, xxxiv). Exploiting this advice, Cicero constructs a history of reference: the dialogue between Crassus and company, the dead heroes of an earlier generation, surveys political, philosophical, and judicial events extending to pre-Socratic Greece, and their constellation of viewpoints is framed by the introductory remarks of a grieving Cicero, himself in retreat from public life and engaged in philosophical nostalgia. Crassus, Antonius, and their friends, all learned in history, law, and philosophy, recall and construe the facts of the past with comparable thoroughness, but cannot agree about what should constitute the education of an orator. Thus Cicero, whose own views on rhetoric and oratory seem divided among the participants in the dialogue, demonstrates that multiple constructions of history, tradition, and the facts are possible, and that the formation of knowledge exploits these possibilities.

The unsettled, sometimes meandering form of *De Oratore* has provoked criticism from those who seem to prefer a more decisive, coherent theory. Such criticism recalls the tendency to disapprove of Plato and Aristotle because they do not allow for a reductive assessment of their works. One of the reasons, surely, that *De Oratore* is not the usual sourcebook for Ciceronian precepts is the quality cited by Richard Whateley, author of a representative nineteenth-century precursor to current-traditional rhetoric, *Elements of Rhetoric*; Whateley complains that Cicero is "adverse to regularity of system and frequently . . . unsatisfactory to the practical student" (7). More recently, M. L. Clark complains of Cicero's philosophical works that "there is much hasty work in them; there are changes of mood which leave us bewildered, and an indifference to consistency which verges on irresponsibility" (54). George Kennedy writes that "the dialogue form has charm, but covers up some real imprecision, for it is entirely too much like a real conversation in which people forget their views for the sake of argument or politeness and in which the general agreement does not represent logical necessity, but either weariness or good manners" (*Art* 226). Once again, such assessments posit coherence and consistency as the virtues of "responsible" philosophy and rhetoric.

Faced with the discursiveness of *De Oratore*, we may—as with the *Phaedrus* and the *Rhetoric*—call it an unsatisfactory treatise, or argue that, despite first impressions, it *is* a well-behaved theoretical statement. Wilbur Samuel Howell does much to identify Cicero with a "Ciceronian formula" and cites *De Oratore* as evidence; explaining that Roman rhetoric consists of five procedures (invention, arrangement, style, memory, delivery), Howell says that "Cicero holds these five procedures as his basic terms . . . as in *De Oratore* and *De Partitione Oratoriae*. . . . Cicero's constant reference to these five terms is a feature of all his writings on rhetoric" (66–67). This reduction of *De Oratore* to a reiteration of Roman recipe rhetoric misrepresents both the scope of Cicero's rhetorical theory and the particular references to the "five terms" in the text. Cicero's treatment of the five parts of classical rhetoric in *De Oratore* is always qualified and ironic. In Book I, xxxi, Crassus speaks of them as the "trite and common precepts of teachers in general"; later in the same book the five parts of rhetoric are mentioned along with other systematic concepts, such as the "motions of the stars," which tend to be reduced to a "science." Here we are warned that "nothing can be reduced to a science" apart from a broad, philosophical conception of the interrelationship of all things (xlii). In such instances, along with the others that Howell cites, Cicero complicates his alliance with Roman rhetoric and its standard principles, so that we may conclude, along with Whateley and contrary to Howell, that Cicero is "adverse to regularity of system."

There is, admittedly, a certain regularity and firmness implied by Cicero's summary of the art of eloquence at the beginning of Book I (v, cited above), as if rhetoric were, indeed, a body of knowledge about history, law, public presentation, and so forth, a body of knowledge that is both finite and objective (at least insofar as the "facts" about history, law, etc. can be stated as such). Cicero reinforces this seeming reification of rhetoric when he discusses memory as "that repository for all things," thus suggesting the synonymy between (excuse the anachronisms) input and output. However, whatever "solid" conception of rhetoric one derives here is immediately complicated once Cicero sets the scene of the dialogue; we realize, for one thing, that memory, "the keeper of the matter and words that are the fruits of thought and invention," is an irresolute faculty:

> *At the time*, then, when the consul Philippus was vehemently inveighing against the cause of the nobility, and the tribune-ship of Drusus, undertaken to support the authority of the senate, seemed to be shaken and weakened, *I was told, I remember*, that Lucius Crassus, *as if for the purpose of collecting his thoughts*, betook himself, during the days of the Roman games, to his Tusculan country seat, whither also Quintus Mucius, who had been his father-in-law, *is said to have come* at the same time, as well as Marcus Antonius, a sharer in all the political proceedings of Crassus, and united in the closest friendship with him. (I, vii, my emphasis)

Here, the Cicero who has touted the importance of history and memory as, respectively, an essential element and an essential faculty of rhetoric, exploits their instability. The layers of recollected narratives that lead Cicero back to the reconstruction of this scene mitigate the "factuality" of the persons and events of the dialogue, but more importantly, call into question the stability of history and memory. We have here Cicero collecting his thoughts about Crassus, who is (ostensibly) collecting his own thoughts, and what lies between Crassus and Cicero is a history of narratives whose questionable proximity to the "truth" accounts for the tentativeness and qualifications emphasized in Cicero's sentence above; matters such as Crassus's purpose for going to the country and the presence of Quintus Mucius are couched as speculations.

While the art of eloquence requires the conjunction of memory and facts, there is, we see here, no stable correspondence between the two. The dialogue of *De Oratore* is, at inception, the creation rather than the recollection of an event, the creation of characters and circumstance demonstrating that memory, the "repository for all things," is a faculty for the invention of narrative and knowledge, not for the storing and retrieval of "facts."

Memory makes meaning, and acts to conjoin multiple perspectives across time. The initial distinction between Cicero and his brother Quintus, between the philosophical orator and the "mechanic" orator, is reiterated and complicated through a "play" of viewpoints throughout the dialogue which are variously associated with either the philosophical or mechanic stance. Thus the intellectual tensions in Cicero's version of the past are fashioned as a commentary on the present. And these voices of a generation ago recall the voices of their own past; early in the dialogue, Antonius recalls a trip to Athens and a dialogue which addresses in large part the same issues that concern Crassus, Antonius, and company (I, xviii–xxi). Speaking in quite general terms that suggest the inevitable imprecision of memory, Antonius recalls his conversation with "most learned men": Mnesarchus, Charmadas, and Menedemus, on the relationship between eloquence, virtue, and philosophy; these Athenians themselves reach still further into the past, citing Demosthenes, Plato, and the "fathers" of rhetoric, Corax and Tisias. Thus shifts in time and geography mix with shifts in viewpoint and interpretation; the dialogue within a dialogue within a dialogue complicates Cicero's pithy, initial distinction between philosophy and utility, and the question of advocating one or the other dissolves in a widening, deepening *drama* of recollections. This activity, the creation of multiple perspectives across time and space, is the foundation for the art of eloquence, which necessarily entails a "vast number of things." If you would be eloquent, Cicero seems to say, do this.

Further, because Antonius's excursion is, of itself, a selective history of rhetoric, reaching back to the originary contributions of Corax and Tisias, it suggests that the history of rhetoric is, like this entire dialogic excursion through the past, the intersection of imperfect and momentous recollections, rather than a stable canon of information. At the beginning of Book III, Cicero reminds us that "I . . . was not present at this dialogue" and explains that all he has available are the "topics and heads of the dissertation" which Cotta (whose own obtuseness during the dialogue makes him a suspect messenger) has supplied.[11]

As Antonius concludes his recollection of the Athens dialogue, the young students, Sulpicius and Cotta, plead for some solid information on eloquence, "something worthy to be remembered"; they regard knowledge as a commodity which can be expressed "fully and exactly" (I, xxi). Faced with the complex instability of memory and history, they want a package deal. What they receive instead, from Crassus especially, is "a multitude of . . . things laid up and heaped together" (I, xxxv). Late in Book I, in an extension of Cicero's claim that the art of eloquence consists of a "vast number of things," Crassus insists that the ideal rhetor must "acquire practice in every thing":

> You must try the strength of your understanding; and your retired lucubrations must be exposed to the light of reality. The poets must also be studied; an acquaintance must be formed with history; the writers and teachers in all the liberal arts and sciences must be read, and turned over, and must for the sake of exercise, be praised, interpreted, corrected, censured, refuted; you must dispute on both sides of every question; and whatever may seem maintainable on any point must be brought forward and illustrated. The civil law must be thoroughly studied; laws in general must be understood;

all antiquity must be known; the usages of the senate, the nature of our government, the rights of our allies, our treaties and conventions, and whatever concerns the interests of the state, must be learned. (I, xxxiv)

At the conclusion of this survey, "a silence ensued." Cicero characterizes the company as both overwhelmed by the force of Crassus's words and frustrated by his lack of precision and detail: ". . . though enough seemed to have been said, in the opinion of the company present, . . . yet they thought that he had concluded his speech more abruptly than they could have wished." Cotta explains this silence by referring to the art of eloquence as an array of objects which Crassus possesses ("that profusion of splendid objects which are his property") and complaining that Crassus has not made his possessions plainly accessible, saying that "I can therefore neither say that I am wholly ignorant of what he possesses, nor that I have plainly ascertained and beheld it" (I, xxv).

Crassus frustrates the desire for knowledge as a (not at all "vast") commodity throughout the three books of *De Oratore*. In Book III, at which point Crassus has been asked to speak on style, he first meditates for two hours, investing what he is about to say with the significance of "causes of the greatest importance," thus suggesting that we should scarcely expect what the auditors desire, a survey of conventional stylistic precepts. And indeed, what Crassus provides is the further association of rhetoric and philosophy and the further derision of academic precepts; all this is couched in sweeping sentences, which, with their relentless embeddings, portray at every turn the mind of a philosopher busy with the "vast number of things" that comprise his art:

> On my authority, therefore, deride and despise all those who imagine that from the precepts of such as are now called rhetoricians they have gained all the powers of oratory, and have not yet been able to understand what character they hold, or what they profess; for indeed, by an orator, every thing that relates to human life, since that is the field on which his abilities are displayed, and is the subject for his eloquence, should be examined, heard, read, discussed, handled, and considered, since eloquence is one of the most

eminent virtues; and though all the virtues are in their nature equal and alike, yet one species is more beautiful and noble than another; as is this power, which comprehending a knowledge of things, expresses the thoughts and purposes of the mind in such a manner that it can compel the audience whithersoever it inclines its force; and, the greater is its influence, the more necessary it is that it should be united with probity and eminent judgment; for if we bestow the faculty of eloquence upon persons destitute of these virtues, we shall not make them orators, but give arms to madmen. (III, xiv)

Punctuating the long survey of Greek philosophy that follows this sentence (xv–xxiii), Crassus once more taunts the tendency to regard knowledge as a readily accessible commodity: "But it is pleasant to be constantly learning, if we wish to be thoroughly masters of any thing; ... And the truth in my opinion is, that a man can never learn thoroughly that which he has not been able to learn quickly." What can be learned quickly—trivial pursuits —stands apart from the art of eloquence which, with all it encompasses, is never-ending.

Once again, Crassus exasperates his auditors, moving Catulus to exclaim, "Now, now," and discount Crassus's discourse as merely idiosyncratic; without contradiction from any of the others, Catulus readily agrees that Crassus should return to the "stated business" of his instruction, a discussion of style *per se*. However, after brief attention to the conventional characteristics of style, Crassus concludes that "every subject, then, has the same susceptibleness of ambiguity" and begins generating questions rooted in such ambiguity that lead him to a discussion, once again, of philosophy and philosophers (xxix–xxxv). Once again, his auditors respond with silence, until Cotta observes that Crassus has been delivering "a dissertation upon a different subject from that on which [he] had undertaken to speak"; Sulpicius adds, angrily, that he "despises" philosophy, and wishes to hear "the ordinary knowledge of common affairs" that will "make some addition to [his] stock of learning" (xxxvi).

Given the tension between Crassus and his auditors throughout *De Oratore*, especially as it is represented by the equally eloquent

Antonius, we must reconsider the tendency—which I have exhibited to some extent already—to isolate Crassus's commentary as representing Cicero's "view" of rhetoric. Aligning Crassus with Cicero reduces the former's pronouncements to "Ciceronian" information and removes them from the dramatic context that has been deliberately created here in order to demonstrate rhetoric as an irresolute interplay of viewpoints. For all his disdain of academic precepts, Crassus knows them well, as he demonstrates with the survey of style and delivery that closes Book III. Further, while Antonius discourages the alignment of rhetoric and philosophy, his dissociation from "learned men" may be a guise: Cicero tells us at the opening of Book II that "Antonius thought that his oratory would be better received by the Roman People if he were believed to have had no learning at all" (i); Antonius says as much later (xxxvii). Further, identifying Cicero exclusively with the pronounced philosophical stance of Crassus discounts the author's mechanistic, academic exposition on humor, via Caesar's monologue, which fills one-fourth of Book II; Caesar's altogether systematic treatment, which categorizes jokes "under a few general heads" (lxxi) meets no objection or complication from any of the other auditors, so we must suppose, at least, that Cicero does not disapprove. Given the difficulty of knowing where Cicero's "own" formulation of rhetorical theory lies, we must be wary to identify Ciceronian rhetoric, in theory and practice, as less than a drama of perspectives.[12]

The philosopher's life of exploration and speculation yields a paradoxical bonus. We learn from Cicero, and even from Aristotle, that the rhetor habitually learning and wondering, the rhetor unconstrained by some purpose or end or stance (the rhetor represented by the unconstrained, variegated form of De Oratore), makes better speeches. Someone like Cicero's Crassus—who reads and writes and investigates constantly—builds up quite a repository of "facts" and develops the suppleness of mind so necessary to constructing what he knows when the occasion arises: the orator "has liberty to expatiate in so large and immense a field and, wherever he stops, can stand upon his own territory" (III, xxxi). A by-product of philosophical rhetoric is the ability to be eloquent on demand.

CHAPTER TWO

Knowledge as Exploration: Montaigne, Vico, Hume

> Who ever asked his pupil what he thinks of rhetoric and grammar, and of such-and-such a saying of Cicero? They slap them into our memory with all their feathers on, like oracles in which the letters and syllables are the substance of the matter.
>
> Montaigne, "Of the Education of Children" (I: xxvi, 112)

The history of rhetoric, as revealed in the· *dicta* of schools and schoolbooks from the Middle Ages through the Enlightenment and beyond, is a series of footnotes to the Ancients. With Plato generally discarded as an "enemy" of rhetoric, Aristotle and Cicero are invoked in the service of formulaic discourse, of rhetoric as technique. The spirit of questing and ambiguity is continued by those who have renegade significance, but scarce influence, in the history of rhetoric: namely, Michel de Montaigne, Giambattista Vico, and David Hume.

Montaigne counters the skeletal logic and ornamental rhetoric encouraged by the prevalent Ciceronianism and emergent Ramism in the Renaissance, rebuking the popular emphasis on style at the expense of invention and imagination (the *Essays* appear in England at about the same time that Francis Bacon's 1605 *Advancement of Learning* warns against the "lawless" activity of free imagination in rhetoric; see especially 146). For Montaigne, generosity of spirit informs writing, and coincides with endless reformulations; writing is "boundless and without form; its food is wonder, the chase, ambiguity. . . . It is an irregular, perpetual motion, without model and without aim. Its inventions excite, pursue, and produce one another" (III: xxii, 818).

Vico succeeds Montaigne, with his eighteenth-century refutation of the popular Cartesian tendencies in rhetoric, logic, and education. In 1708, when Vico delivers his address *On the Study Methods of Our Time* at the University of Naples, Descartes' mechanistic view of language and learning has swept Europe.[1] Just as Descartes' *Discourse*, with its faith in mathematical reason, is a denial of Montaigne's *Essays*, so Vico's renovation of the creative intellect affronts the *Discourse*. Mindful that "human events are dominated by Chance and Choice," Vico dismisses the "clear and distinct perception" valorized by Descartes for a more complex and unsettled vision of rhetoric; locating oneself within a variegated reality requires the "capacity to perceive the analogies existing between matters lying far apart and, apparently, most dissimilar" (24). Vico's later, larger work, *The New Science*, demonstrates most extensively his involvement in the tangle of associational thinking that is the root of community.

Later in the eighteenth century, in Great Britain, David Hume recalls Vico and Montaigne as he explains the intellectual power to associate impressions and ideas. Hume repeatedly insists that the associative power of the mind frees us to question and revise matters taken for granted, to create new perspectives. One of the central statements of Hume's skepticism, "Whatever *is*, may not be," is tied to his belief in the primacy of intellectual free play: "Nothing is more free than the imagination of man . . . it has unlimited power of mixing, compounding, separating, and dividing [matters of fact] in all the varieties of fiction and vision" (*Works* IV, 40). Once we consider Hume's philosophy as a rhetorical theory, what emerges is his increasing admiration for unconventional ideas embodied in such imaginative juxtapositions.

The views of Montaigne, Vico, and Hume maintain the equivalence of rhetoric and intellectual free play through the centuries when rhetoric became a mechanized ornament of thought and critical thinking became schematized. Muffled by the rationalist voice of mainstream technical rhetoric, these thinkers have been dissociated from the rhetorical tradition, although, as I will propose, they continue the Ancient emphasis on rhetoric as philosophy, and look toward the postmodern alliance of language, literacy, and open speculation.

Montaigne, *Essays*

Montaigne expanded and revised his *Essays* continually, from 1572 through 1588; by inventing the essay as an "endless" activity, he carries forward the demonstration of philosophical rhetoric—as an art of wondering—begun in Antiquity. The *Essays* are latticed with hundreds of references to Plato, Aristotle, and Cicero, which taken together submit a classical patrimony of fallible minds whose "authority" is subject to play, whose philosophy and rhetoric generate (rather than foreclose) more philosophy and rhetoric. Presenting us with the "Master of Arts" whose talk is full of "commentaries," who would "beat our ears with pure and undigested Aristotle" (III: viii, 707), Montaigne ridicules the tendency to parrot the pronouncements of Antiquity. He charges with ignorance those who remove classical texts from the patchwork and motley of the self and the world and the common sense, those for whom knowledge is a distilled essence rather than a fluctuant experience: "I have run my eyes over a certain dialogue of Plato [the *Phaedrus*], a fantastic motley in two parts, the beginning part about love, all the rest about rhetoric. The ancients do not fear these changes, and with wonderful grace they let themselves be tossed in the wind, or seem to" (III: ix, 761).

For Montaigne, Plato is a "disconnected poet," who shows us that "all things are in perpetual flux, change, and variation" (II: 12, 455):

The leader of his dialogues, Socrates, is always asking questions and stirring up discussion, never concluding, never satisfying. . . . From Plato arose ten different sects, they say. And indeed, in my opinion, never was teaching wavering and

noncommital if his is not. . . . Plato seems to me to have
favored this form of philosophizing [to inquire rather than
to instruct] in dialogues deliberately, to put more fittingly in
diverse mouths the diversity and variation of his own ideas.
(II: xii, 377)

Denying Platonic philosophy either preeminence or consistency,
Montaigne cites Plato as a commentator on pain and pleasure,
weaponry, boxing, the soul, death, dreams, health, excessive sleep,
excessive drinking, purgations, euthanasia, doctors, illness, medi-
cine, servants and servitude, love, lawyers, exercise, beauty, good
humor, justice, sex, the suitability of body parts in marriage part-
ners, the art of argument, the art of style, the art of government,
and truthfulness. Plato is one of the "patchmakers" (III: xii, 808)
whose broad curiosity affords Montaigne a range of "borrowings,"
so that he may give each "some particular application with my
own hand, so that it may be less purely someone else's . . . we
naturalists judge that the honor of invention is greatly and incom-
parably preferable to the honor of quotation" (III: xii, 809). Invention means "piling up" perspectives. Montaigne reads Plato to
borrow, or displace, quotations and ideas from Plato's discourse
in order to replace them among materials from other sources. The
resultant medley constitutes a new patchwork. Thus, Plato joins
Montaigne's meditation on the relationship between the body and
the soul:

> Aristippus defended the body alone, as if we had no soul;
> Zeno embraced only the soul, as if we had no body. Both
> were wrong. Pythagoras, they say, followed a philosophy that
> was all contemplation, Socrates one that was all conduct and
> action; Plato found the balance between the two. But they
> say so to make a good story, and the true balance is found
> in Socrates, and Plato is much more Socratic than Pytha-
> gorean, and it becomes him better. (III: xiii, 850)

In such passages, so typical of the *Essays*, writing—as philosophy
—is an assemblage of borrowings from earlier assemblages. Thus
Montaigne continues, more overtly, the philosophical rhetoric begun in the "fantastic motley" of Plato's *Phaedrus*, with its dialectical

patchwork of multiple voices. Such rhetoric creates the "self" which is the "subject" of Montaigne's writing, the self which, "in all things and throughout, is but patchwork and motley" (II: xx, 511).

As another examplar of the excursive rhetoric and philosophy that Montaigne exploits, Aristotle "discusses and stirs up everything" (I: iii, 10). However, obeisance to Aristotle as the "monarch of modern learning" (I: xxvi, 107) has reduced this philosopher who (like Montaigne) "ordinarily piles up for us a great number of other opinions and other beliefs" (II: xii, 376) to a dogmatist whose words are memorized by fools:

> I had a private talk with a man at Pisa, a good man, but such an Aristotelian that the most sweeping of his dogmas is that the touch-stone and measure of all solid speculation and of all truth is conformity with the teaching of Aristotle; that outside of this there is nothing but chimeras and inanity; that Aristotle saw everything and said everything. (I: xxvi, 111)

Like the boy Phaedrus in Plato's dialogue, this man does not realize that "only the fools are certain and assured," and in his uncritical devotion to Aristotle's precepts, he disregards philosophy as a *way of thinking*; as Montaigne warns, "He who follows another follows nothing. . . . He must imbibe their ways of thinking, not learn their precepts." While Aristotle's principles are "in vogue" (II: xii, 429), the philosophical ambiguity of his writing cannot be appreciated; however, attention to the "way of thinking" that Aristotle offers redefines his writing as a collection of possibilities. Playing with the definition of God, Montaigne includes Aristotle's several characterizations among his own several dozen: "Aristotle says now that it is the mind, now the world; now he gives this world another master, and now makes God the heat of heaven" (II: 12, 382). Thus Montaigne portrays the Aristotle of the *Rhetoric* who argues for open exploration while he traverses options.

Cicero stands with Plato and Aristotle as a classical figure whose words are but mouthed by pedants:

> Just as birds sometimes go in quest of grain, and carry it in their beak without tasting it to give a beakful to their little

ones, so our pedants go pillaging knowledge in books and lodge it only on the end of their lips, in order merely to disgorge it and scatter it to the winds. . . . We know how to say: "Cicero says thus; such are the morals of Plato; these are the very words of Aristotle." But what do we say our- selves? What do we judge? What do we do? A parrot could well say as much. (I: xxv, 100)

Later, Montaigne adds, "I would rather be an authority on myself than on Cicero" (III: 13, 822), suggesting both the primacy of self- expression over "pillaged" knowledge, and some disdain for "the father of Roman eloquence" (II: x, 299). Seeking to make Cicero his own, and "imbibe" his ways of thinking, Montaigne admits difficulty. Apart from the works that "treat of philosophy," he has no use for the "prefaces, definitions, partitions, [and] etymologies" which "consume the greater part" of Cicero's work (II: x, 301). It is the schematic Cicero, of "logical and Aristotelian arrange- ments," whose motives for writing Montaigne calls vainglorious, and whose style is "boring" (I: x1, *passim*).

Montaigne's place in the sixteenth-century anti-Ciceronian movement is surveyed briefly in Morris Croll's much cited 1923 discussion of Attic prose. Croll notes that Montaigne "effected his escape from the humanistic orthodoxy" and became "the pioneer in a new phase of modern thought" by virtue of his "libertine prose" (178). While dismissing the aridity of Ciceronian style, and discrediting Cicero's formulary tendencies, Montaigne also makes Cicero a philosophical skeptic as he argues for the value of a rhetoric of uncertainty in the "Apology for Raymond Sebond." In a late revision of this essay, Montaigne includes Cicero as a spokes- person for Pyrrhonian skepticism; according to Montaigne's Cicero,

This method in philosophy of arguing against everything and making no open judgment of anything, started by Socrates, repeated by Arcesilaus, confirmed by Carneades, flourishes still even in our time. We are those who say that some falsehood is mixed with every truth, with so much similarity that there is no criterion in them by which we can judge and assent with certainty. (II: xii, 376)

Montaigne here places Cicero among the skeptics, including Aristotle, who recognize that "knowing much gives occasion for doubting more," and practice "Pyrrhonism in an affirmative form." The preeminent Cicero of constrictive principles and precepts gives way to a philosophical Cicero patched into Montaigne's intellectual history.

While he prompts the reintegration of classical voices into the discourse of skepticism, Montaigne rejects rhetoric that aims to exploit "the stupidity and facility that is found in the common people." Rhetoric that would manipulate and manage public knowledge, rather than examine and interrogate, is a "lying and deceitful art" (I: li, 221–22). However, Montaigne's "position" on rhetoric and writing is more complex and inconclusive than such adamant pronouncements suggest. His castigation of "lying and deceitful" rhetoric conceals his own deceit, the practice of dislocating and complicating and ambiguating revered authority, established beliefs, and common knowledge, so that we are at pains to say when and how and where in his essay the truth *lies*. Significantly, Montaigne's central question, "What do I know?" emerges from his emphasis on the deceitful power of language:

> Most of the occasions for the troubles of the world are grammatical. . . . Let us take the sentence that logic itself offers us as the clearest. If you say "It is fine weather," and if you are speaking the truth, then it is fine weather. Isn't that a sure way of speaking? Still it will deceive us. To show this let us continue the examples. If you say "I lie," and if you are speaking the truth, then you lie. The art, the reason, the force of the conclusion of this one are the same as in the other; yet there we are stuck in the mud.
>
> I can see why the Pyrrhonians cannot express their general conception in any manner of speaking, for they would need a new language. Ours is wholly formed of affirmative propositions, which to them are utterly repugnant; so that when they say "I doubt," immediately you have them by the throat to make them admit that at least they know and are sure of this fact, that they doubt. Thus they have been constrained to take refuge in this comparison from medicine, without

which their attitude would be inexplicable: when they declare "I do not know" or "I doubt," they say that this proposition carries itself away with the rest, no more nor less than rhubarb, which expels evil humors and carries itself off with them.

This idea is more firmly grasped in the form of interrogation: "What do I know?" (II: xii, 392–93)

The instability of linguistic meaning makes lying and deceit —in the guise of affirmation—inevitable. Admitting this means refusing to affirm a singular view, entertaining a succession of perspectives, making discourse "an irregular perpetual motion, without model and without aim." Sensitive to the "lying and deceitful art" of rhetoric as an insistence upon clear and distinct ideas, Montaigne refuses to lie by refusing to conclude, by exploiting the very scope and liberty of his *Essays*. As Victoria Kahn has observed, "the more interesting and more radical criticism of rhetoric is found not in [Montaigne's] thematic statements, but in the form and practice . . . of the essay itself" (115). "Of Coaches" represents the excursive form and practice, with its implicit critique, that Kahn cites. Montaigne begins by defining "great authors" as those who "pile up" the possible "causes" of phenomena:

It is very easy to demonstrate that great authors, when they write about causes, adduce not only those they think are true but also those they do not believe in, provided they have some originality and beauty. They speak truly and usefully enough if they speak ingeniously. We cannot make sure of the master cause; we pile up several of them, to see if by chance it will be found among them,

For one cause will not do;
We must state many, one of which is true.
Lucretius (III: vi, 685)

Then, as if beginning to illustrate Lucretius's words, Montaigne wonders "whence comes this custom of blessing those who sneeze," speculates on one cause of such blessing, but quickly leaves considerations of head, nose, and cold-sickness to examine stomach-sickness: "the reason for the heaving of the stomach that affects those who travel by sea." Proposing fear as the cause of seasickness, Montaigne essays at some length the causes and consequences of fear, leaving off to reconsider motion sickness, particularly the motion sickness he suffers in coaches. Now motion sickness merges with fear as another of the "weaknesses that are in me," and the plague of coach-motion is set aside for a note on how coaches have been used through history "in the service of war," or we might say, on the fields of fear. The interanimation of sickness, fear, coaches, and war leads to a brief focus on the vehicles of monarchs, and the particular recollection that "the Emperor Firmus had his chariot drawn by ostriches of marvelous size," which provokes Montaigne's self-conscious reversion to historical examples of royal ostentation: "The strangeness of these inventions [ostrich-drawn chariots, and so forth] puts into my head this other notion: that it is a sort of pusillanimity in monarchs, and evidence of not sufficiently feeling what they are, to labor at showing off and making a display by excessive expense" (667–68). The problem of royal ostentation at public expense leads to the issue of liberality—the virtues and vices of royal gift-giving. Surveying the extravagances of past monarchs and cultures, Montaigne marvels at the practices of "minds different from ours" and complains of our "puny and limited" knowledge of other worlds: "If we saw as much of the world as we do not see, we would perceive, it is likely, a perpetual multiplication and vicissitude of forms" (693). Then follows a long summary of events in the new American world just discovered, emphasizing Montaigne's fascination with the ways of the Mexican natives. Finally, with a bow to earlier subjects of this essay, Montaigne touches upon the "pomp and magnificence" of the roads and palaces in the new world and concludes by noting that no one there rides in coaches: "Instead of these or any other form of transport, [kings] had themselves carried by men . . . (699).

With its movement through the permutations of an intellectual landscape in which sickness, fear, war, travel, ostentation, liberality, royalty, and foreign practices are contiguous and unfixed markers for the appearance of anecdotes, facts, complaints, and "cadged" quotations, "Of Coaches" denies any expository summary that presumes "matters of fact" and demonstrates Montaigne's explicit insistence upon knowledge-as-exploration, not knowledge-as-information. The distinction between exploration and information is pressed in Montaigne's two "pedagogical" essays, "Of Pedantry" and "Of the Education of Children." In both, Montaigne scoffs at the wasted time teachers and students spend schematizing knowledge through writing:

> They keep us for four or five years learning to understand words and stitch them into sentences; as many more, to mold them into a great body, extending into four or five parts; and another five, at least, learning how to mix and interweave them briefly in some subtle way. (I: xxvi, 124–25)

Montaigne's pupil has no use for such exercises; he "does not know rhetoric," but is "well-equipped with substance," that is, the spacious intelligence of the philosophical mind, so that "words will follow only too readily" (I: xxvi, 125). "Of Pedantry," with its severe appraisal of knowledge-as-information and its suspended conclusion, exhibits the "substance" Montaigne would cultivate in students. My summary of this essay preserves Montaigne's point-of-view:

> As a child, I was annoyed and confused that teachers were treated with ridicule and contempt. As an adult, I too find them contemptible, but wonder why this is true of minds with so much knowledge. Perhaps, as I was told, learning crowds the brain rather than improves it. Perhaps, "as plants are stifled with too much moisture, and lamps with too much oil, so too much study and matter stifles the action of the mind." But this isn't always true: knowledge can fill up the soul; examples are great and learned public men from the past.
>
> Learned private men—philosophers—are ridiculed for being apart from the "common herd." The Platonic picture of the philosopher, "envied as being above the common fashion," is far removed from the present view of philosophers as base and incapable. In the past, some philosophers were great public men. Others set themselves "above fortune and

the world" and led "base and necessitous lives." I think such
men are neither wise nor prudent.

There is a better explanation for the deficiencies of learned
men. These pedants merely pillage knowledge from books,
and like birds, give an untasted "beakful" of it to students,
who receive it uncritically and without conscience (I am a
pillager too, of a sort!). We parrot the knowledge of others,
and ignore our own minds and bodies. This habit reminds
me of a rich Roman who surrounded himself with learned
men who gave him knowledge on demand; another man can't
even complain about his "itchy backside" without looking
up these words in a book. We must make our knowledge
our own.

Pedants do not improve the souls of their students: "they
have a full enough memory but an entirely hollow judgment."
Judgment (moral and practical application) is more valuable
than learning (storing information). Maybe this is because
learning makes no money, except for schoolmasters, who are
of the "basest alloy" and incompetent for a better living.
Making souls fit means teaching the elements of virtue, which
are learned from deeds, not precepts and words. In Sparta,
children learned, not rhetoric and dialectic, but "the finest
science there is, the science of obeying and commanding."

"The pursuit of knowledge makes men's hearts soft and
effeminate more than it makes them strong and warlike."
Witness the Turks, who despise letters; or pre-literate Rome;
or the crude and ignorant Scythians, Parthians, Goths; or the
French conquest of the learned but soft people of Naples and
Tuscany. (I: xxv, 97–106)

One rhetorical figure that may describe the "substance" of Montaigne's variegated form and content in this essay and others is
antithesis. Through "Of Pedantry" Montaigne presents what Valesio has called "psychological fluctuations between pairs of oppo-
sites" (e.g., past/present, public knowledge/private knowledge,
weakness/strength, mind/body), and thus portrays "one of the basic
ways of perceiving the world" (Valesio 126). Identifying this tendency in Montaigne as a "Sophist technique" also evident in Aristotle's *Rhetoric*, Valesio proposes "the primacy of antithesis as the

rhetorical figure that best expresses the dialectical nature of rhetorical structures" which are "the inescapable ways of expressing conflicts in real life" (103).

Recognizing antithesis as a structural token of knowledge-as-exploration, we must add that Montaigne avoids the philosophical resolution of antitheses, that is, synthesis: in "Of Pedantry" he "piles up" some "causes" of the puzzling fact that "the greatest scholars are not the wisest men," until barbarians appear as a possible antithesis to pedants; at this point Montaigne—as if to shrug "What do I know?"—stops, leaving to us the conciliation of a schoolmaster and a Goth.

Insisting upon philosophical writing as a collocation of perspectives, or structure of disjunctions, without absolute terms, Montaigne's "thematic" statements repeatedly discourage those who would extract some generative principle of composition from the Essays, insisting that his discourse is "termless and formless" and reflects the irreducible complexities of the writerly self:

> Not only does the wind of accident move me at will, but, besides, I am moved and disturbed as a result merely of my own unstable posture; and anyone who observes carefully can hardly find himself twice in the same state. I give my soul now one face, now another, according to which direction I turn it. If I speak of myself in different ways, that is because I look at myself in different ways. All contradictions may be found in me by some twist and in some fashion. Bashful, insolent; chaste, lascivious; talkative, taciturn; tough, delicate; clever, stupid; surly, affable; lying, truthful; learned, ignorant; liberal, miserly, and prodigal: all this I see in myself to some extent according to how I turn; and whoever studies himself really attentively finds in himself, yes, even in his judgment, this gyration and discord. I have nothing to say about myself absolutely, simply, and solidly, without confusion and without mixture, or in one word. (II: i, 242)

Vico and Hume counterpose the rhetoric of the discordant self to the emergence of positivistic science. Like Montaigne, these philosophers argue against the primacy of the "clear and distinct idea"; unlike Montaigne, they each develop a terminology which, in effect, countermands the absolutist terminology informing science, logic, and rhetoric. In Vico and Hume, then, we are offered a lexicon for describing rhetoric as an art of wondering.

Vico, *On the Study Methods of Our Time*

When he was seven years old, Giambattista Vico fell on his head. It was predicted he would either die or grow up to be an idiot. He grew up to be a professor of rhetoric; significantly, a renegade professor of rhetoric. Vico claims that the knock on the head contributed to his intellectual powers: "As a result of this mischance, [I] grew up with a melancholy and irritable temperament such as belongs to men of ingenuity and depth, who, thanks to the one, are quick as lightning in perception, and thanks to the other, take no pleasure in verbal cleverness or falsehood" (*Autobiography* 111). For Vico, ingenuity and depth are the elements of philosophical imagination, and here he associates the birth of such imagination with discontent, initiated by a great and painful jolt.

In the work for which he is best known, *The New Science*, Vico also associates the beginning of human imagination with a severe shock, the first burst of lightning and thunder on the dark sky. According to Vico's fable, primitive people must have responded to the first thunderstorm with astonishment and fear, with passionate shouting and wonder about what was happening in the sky. They picture, quite literally *imagine*, the unknown in terms of the known; they picture the source of the storm in terms of themselves, as a superhuman being, a divine image of man, a god (¶377).

This originary act, of defining humanity in terms of divinity, represents for Vico why and how the imagination creates and maintains *sensus communis*, or common sense. Imagination is provoked by discontent—by astonished ignorance, in this case—and becomes unnecessary and useless once certainty (with all its comforts) takes over. Imagination has no place in a world where "pedantic meticulousness" (*Study Methods* 65) holds sway.

While he wrote and revised *The New Science*, Vico was professor of rhetoric at the University of Naples. And even after his labor of more than twenty years, *The New Science* remains incomplete, fragmentary, at once tangled and profound; it represents work-in-progress even in its final 1744 version, less a conclusive piece of philosophy or history than the artifact of persistent invention and revision. Thus *The New Science* embodies Vico's own conception of rhetoric, which is, as Donald Verene points out, "an activity in which the mind constructs a knowledge of itself" (*Vico's Science of Imagination* 165), in which one constitutes what Vico calls a "mental dictionary," a lexicon of associations that locates the human intellect in human history.

Essentially, *The New Science* explicates the development of consciousness through the three ages of man. Verene summarizes this Vichian history most succinctly:

> In Vico's ideal eternal history there are three ages: the age in which men thought *in terms of gods*, the age in which men thought *in terms of heroes*, and the age of purely human understanding. The third age is barbaric because it is an age of purely reflective thinking . . . in which we have no contact with divination or heroic narration as the means of wisdom. ("The New Art of Narration" 25, my emphasis).

Vico's third age regresses toward the end of society and the subsequent dissolution of humankind. Civilization stops when we cease to think metaphorically and associatively, cease to ponder one thing *in terms of* others, cease to see each human life as a tangle of relationships to divinity and history and the common sense. In other words, civilization stops when we trade philosophical imagination for intellectual purity, when we trade the unstable world of human affairs for the deep solitude of certainty.

Until the middle of this century, when full English translations of Vico's major statements began to appear, his work had attracted scarce attention from Anglo-American scholars; now a great Vico industry exists, celebrating *The New Science* in particular as a harbinger of contemporary thought. However, scholarship in the history of rhetoric mentions Vico only in passing, if at all: standard reference works ignore him altogether (e.g., Kennedy, Horner) or reduce his work to a set of precepts (Golden, et al.). Michael Mooney has helped to redress this lack of attention with his recent book, *Vico in the Tradition of Rhetoric*, where he admits that the "fertility of the rhetorical tradition . . . remains largely an untold story. When it comes to be told in full, it is clear that Vico must occupy a significant chapter" (19).

In one early speech recognized now as a foundation for *The New Science*, Vico explains the role of education in the future of imagination and community. This speech, *On the Study Methods of Our Time*, was Vico's seventh annual address, inaugurating the opening of studies at the University of Naples in 1708. Against Cartesian rationalism, which amounts to sterile intellection for Vico, he posits the philosophical imagination, which is the capacity to connect "matters lying far apart," that is, the capacity to think metaphorically.[2]

In *Study Methods*, Vico fears that adolescents trained in Cartesian analytics, with mathematical theorems as the foundation of pure truth, learn one narrow procedure for *judging* ideas, but are left without the ability to generate them. He declares that such training, "the main purpose of which is to cleanse its fundamental truth not only of all falsity, but also of the mere suspicion of error . . . is distinctly harmful, since training in common sense is essential to the education of adolescents, so that the faculty should be developed as early as possible; else they break into odd or arrogant behavior when adulthood is reached" (13). In sum, training in the judgment of truth and falsehood is inimical to common sense, once we understand common sense as a complex of shared judgments, a complex that is always changing, a complex that is, in a word, rhetorical. The development of common sense, then, is the enlargement of the capacity to express what is probably true at the time.

Vico is aware that the invention of probable truths—as it is discussed in its most supple terms by Aristotle and the mature Cicero—has lost an honorable place in philosophy and rhetoric: "The art of 'topics,' far from being given first place in the curriculum, is utterly disregarded. . . . this is harmful, since the invention of arguments is by nature prior to the judgment of their validity, so that, in teaching, that invention should be given priority over [analysis]" (14). Those trained in formulaic analysis and judgment, at the expense of invention, become either meek or arrogant; they either "accept any viewpoint [that] has been sanctioned by a teacher," or "step rashly into discussions while they are still in the process of learning" (19). Intellectual sheep or intellectual bullies. They are capable of only "the geometrical kind of exposition," a linear sequence of prescribed and predictable steps, rather than the "ample manner of utterance," that intellectual versatility associated with the interconnection of different lines of thought, with eloquence.

Significantly, invention is not a *technique*, with all the narrow implications of that term. Invention is the habit of a mind constantly gathering, sorting, synthesizing, *not* to arrive at any final solution or truth, but to make decisions "in the field of action, which, in the course of time, prove to be as profitable as the nature of things permits" (35). Invention is the habit of the active philosopher, buffeted by the unstable, mutable phenomena of human life. For philosophers-in-life, excellence is accorded not to those who formulate and finalize conclusions, but to those who "ferret out the greatest possible number of causes which may have produced a single event, and who are able to conjecture which of all these causes is the true one" (34), mindful that truth is always a contingent term.

The contingency of truth in human affairs, implicit throughout *Study Methods*, is stated more directly by Vico in *On the Ancient Wisdom of the Italians*, published in 1710. Here Vico explains the *verum-factum* principle: simply stated, "The true is what is made." Thus, the only intelligence capable of absolute knowledge is God, "because God is the first maker." Divine truth is "solid," while human truth is "what man arranges and makes as he knows it" (*Selected Writings* 50–52). Knowing is making, in the world of human affairs.

With this assumption, and his elaboration of it in *Study Methods*, Vico revives the identification of philosophy and rhetoric that informs classical thought. He recalls the emphasis of Aristotle and Cicero on the rhetor's development of philosophical imagination, on the elaboration of perspectives that makes eloquence possible. With the reduction of Aristotle and Cicero to textbook formulas for rhetoric students through the Middle Ages, and the delimitation of rhetoric to stylistic elegance after 1500, Vico's renewal of classical rhetoric as the nexus of uncertainty and method does seem, as Michael Mooney has noted, "reactionary" (69). I represent the elements of Vico's *Study Methods* in the chart on page 61, to begin a more pointed discussion of his conjunction of imagination, invention, and eloquence, and to suggest the fertile classicism he recalls.

The Elements of Vico's Study Methods

	TRAINED PERCEPTION OF	A SENSE OF	COMMON
EXPERIENCE	RELATIONSHIPS	PROBABILITIES	SENSE
Memory	Topics		
Wonder	Ingenuity		
Ignorance			
Discontent			ELOQUENCE

Experience

Invention is informed by memory and provoked by wonder. Memory is a particularly troublesome term in Vico's work, since it means not only a sense impression as such, but also names the forming power of the imagination:

> Just as old age is powerful in reason, so is adolescence in imagination. . . . Furthermore, the teacher should give the greatest care to the cultivation of the pupil's memory, which, though not exactly the same as imagination is almost identical with it. . . . Youth's natural inclination to the arts in which imagination or memory (or a combination of both) is prevalent (such as painting, poetry, oratory, jurisprudence) should by no means be blunted. (14)

To the school subjects listed here, in which students create and conjoin images and concepts, Vico adds geometry, not as an analytic study, but as exercise in the "vivid capacity to form images" that illustrate logical relationships.

The conflation of imagination and memory is further explained in *The New Science*:

> Memory thus has three different aspects: memory when it remembers things, imagination when it alters or imitates

them, and invention when it gives them a new turn or puts them into proper arrangement or relationship. (¶819)

By enlarging the definition of memory, here and in *Study Methods*, Vico transforms an abandoned element of formulary rhetoric. Since the second century, memory had been discussed in textbooks as one of the five parts of rhetoric (along with invention, arrangement, style, and delivery); in this context, memory was synonymous with memorization, and allied to artificial devices for memorizing a speech. Because of both a shift away from memorized oratory, and the Renaissance "reform" of rhetoric that excluded both memory and invention, by Vico's time memory was not the concern of rhetoricians and was employed by students of Cartesian philosophy merely for reiterating the "constant and gradual series of small, closely concatenated steps" of analytical exposition (*Study Methods* 24). The irrelevance of memorization in post-classical rhetoric is punctuated in this century by Edward P. J. Corbett in his famous recapitulation of classical precepts, *Classical Rhetoric for the Modern Student*, in which he completely excludes *memoria*. However, memory reconsidered in its Vichian associations becomes an element that cannot be dismissed from a modern, generative rhetoric. Memory is not merely the replication of experience; it is for Vico experience imagined and invented, altered and arranged, recollected and re-associated; it is the foundation of Montaigne's "patchwork." Memory is a faculty that makes experience.

Experience becomes the resource of imagination and invention under the aegis of wonder, attendant to ignorance, discontent, and fear. Vico prefers a state of uncertainty to Descartes' "clear and distinct idea" throughout *Study Methods*, and the *quality* of uncertainty that provokes the making of meaning is proposed in the *Autobiography* and *The New Science*. Recall that Vico's *Autobiography* begins by connecting a melancholy and irritable temperament with "ingenuity and depth." In other words, contemplation springs from a chafed sensibility. In *The New Science*, Vico tells of primitives terrorized and confused by the thunderstorm, provoked to name the unknown: "And thus they began to exercise that natural curiosity, which is the daughter of ignorance and the mother of knowledge, and which, opening the mind of man, gives birth to

wonder" (¶377). Thought originates in a mind profoundly unsettled, in chaos, in the dark.

Trained Perception of Relationships

Vico says in *Study Methods* that "criticism is the art of speaking
truly, topics of speaking copiously."[3] By criticism he means Cartesian analytics, which allow one to speak truly, but only within the
confines of the closed system. Topics are questions and considerations that fill out a copious "mental encyclopedia" of perspectives; they are the elements of intellectual versatility. Vico's extensive
discussion of topics in *On the Ancient Wisdom of the Italians* complements his advocacy in *Study Methods*: he proposes that only
through topical exploration can one approach clarity. Paradoxically,
Vico's sketch of the questioning mind makes closure and clarity
seem distant ideals indeed:

> For how can a clear and distinct idea in our mind be a
> criterion of the true unless we perceive everything in, or
> related to, the thing itself? And how can anyone be certain
> that he has perceived everything, unless he has pursued every
> question pertaining to the matter under consideration? First
> [he should raise] the question whether it exists, lest he should
> be talking about nothing. Then the question what it is, lest
> his efforts be expended upon a name. Then how great it is,
> whether in extent, weight or number. Then what it is like,
> under which heading come color, taste, softness, hardness
> and the other tactile sensations. Then he must ask when it
> was created, how long it lasts, and into what it changes as
> it decays. And proceeding thus through the remaining cat-
> egories, he must connect it to all the things which are in any
> way related to it, whether they be its causes or effects, or
> those effects it has when combined with objects which are
> similar, dissimilar or contrary, or when combined with those
> which are bigger, smaller, or equal. . . . On the other hand,
> anyone who is confident of perceiving something in a clear
> and distinct idea of the mind is easily deceived, and he will
> often think that he knows a thing distinctly when he still

has only a confused consciousness of it, for he has not learned
all the elements which belong to the object and which distinguish it from everything else. (*Selected Writings* 72–73)

Significantly, the topics are essentially metaphorical: they require
considering the subject *in terms of* something else, in terms of
comparison or effect, for instance. Thus, insofar as they promote
associative thinking, topics draw from the "specifically philosophic
faculty" of the student.

Vico does not associate topics with the mere enumeration of
data, but rather with the raising of questions. Topical philosophy,
the process of finding arguments, has primacy over rational philosophy, which settles them. Furthermore, Vico's survey of the
questions one might raise establishes the endless possibilities for
inquiry, given a context of mutable relationships. Thus he reaffirms
the classical identification of rhetoric with inquiry.

However, Vico admits, the appeal of clarity and certainty
seems universal. With his tongue-in-cheek tribute to modern science in *Study Methods*, Vico both echoes contemporary approbation
and suggests that the enthusiastic welcoming of scientistic rationalism is thoughtless, empty bombast:

What cannot be denied is the fact that leading investigators
have available to them a science enriched by a number of
new and ingenious discoveries. Modern scientists, seeking for
guidance in their exploration of the dark pathways of nature,
have introduced the geometrical method into physics. Holding to this method as to Ariadne's thread, they can reach
the end of their appointed journey. Do not consider them
as groping practitioners of physics: they are to be viewed,
instead, as the grand architects of this limitless fabric of the
world: able to give a detailed account of the ensemble of
principles according to which God has built this admirable
structure of the cosmos. . . . Almost all of these spheres of
mental activity have as their single goal the inquiry after
truth. Were I to set out to extol this inquiry, I would arouse
wonder at my eulogizing something that no one ever thought
of disparaging. (9–11)

Aware of Vico's bitter opposition to the "geometrical method" (i.e., Cartesian analytics) throughout *Study Methods* and elsewhere, we understand the irony of these introductory paragraphs. Those who celebrate the narrow inquiry after God's "ensemble of principles" are incapable of critical thinking about their own enterprise, immersed in a culture where no disparaging voice is raised against the imperfect pursuit of perfect truth.

For Vico, the art of topics is a mode of resisting *a priori* conclusions, of avoiding the blindness of one's own culture. To the elaboration of topics Vico's student brings ingenuity, an inborn power that "consists in the yoking of different things." Ingenuity "calls up" or "discovers" a connection between terms; it is the power of associative thinking. Vico implies the presence of ingenuity in his own discourse at the same time as he denigrates the importance of fixed goals or "aims" in education. He raises the issue of what the aim of contemporary study should be, and where he will address such aims in his own text:

> As for the aim, it should circulate, like a blood-stream, through the entire body of the learning process. Consequently, just as the blood's pulsation may best be studied at the spot where the arterial beat is most perceptible, so the aim of our study methods shall be treated at the point where it assumes the greatest prominence. (6)

Vico refuses to preestablish some "end" for learning and associates both learning and writing—his own discourse—with a journey that is regular and regulated but "aimless." The progress of study is compared to a recursive rather than a linear process, whose aims emerge during that process itself. Here we detect Vico's trust in ingenuity, in the natural tendency to arrive at points of clarity, of acute consciousness. Vico implicitly associates learning with discovery.[4]

Probabilities, Common Sense, and Eloquence

Training in the perception of relationships teaches that there are multiple ways of naming, or narrating, experience. The probable causes, or effects, of any phenomenon are many. In *The New Science,* Vico says, "there were as many Joves, with as many names, as there were nations" (¶379). A sense of probabilities, of multiple ways of naming and knowing that stretch across time and space, allows one to determine the *sensus communis*, or common sense. As with so many of Vico's central terms, the meaning of "common sense" is extensive and ambiguous. He tells us in *The New Science* that "common sense is judgment *without reflection*, shared by an entire class, an entire people, an entire nation, or the entire human race" (¶142). And in *Study Methods* Vico proposes that common sense is the nexus of invention and eloquence:

> It is a positive fact that, just as knowledge originates in truth and error in falsity, so common sense arises from perceptions based on verisimilitude. . . . I may add that common sense, besides being the criterion of practical judgment, is also the guiding standard of eloquence. . . . There is a danger that instruction in advanced philosophical criticism [Cartesian analytics] may lead to an abnormal growth of abstract intellectualism, and render young people unfit for the practice of eloquence. (13)

The multiplication of probabilities enlarges common sense by enlarging the common ground of human activity. For instance, in *The New Science*, Vico is developing "the common nature of nations," that is, the core beliefs and rituals (i.e., belief in God, marriage, and burial of the dead) which inform language, culture, and imagination, which are maintained through all the permutations of history. It is this large "common sense," derived from a study of *life*, that trivializes the small, closed, Cartesian realm of abstract rules and symbols, removed from the vital tangle of human relationships.

Eloquence requires sensitivity to the particular common sense one is addressing. Vico offers the now rather familiar advice that we must arrange our speech "in tune with the opinions of the audience" (15). The important point is that eloquence—which was for Vico's students the practice of effective and *spontaneous* oratory—is automatic if the speaker's common sense is large and inclusive, and impossible otherwise; the speaker must be like Montaigne's pupil, "well equipped with substance." Vico speaks of those orators who are not practiced at surveying perspectives, at topical invention:

> Individuals who have not achieved this ability hardly deserve the name of orators. In pressing urgent affairs ... it is the orator's business to give *immediate* assistance to the accused, who is usually granted only a few hours to plead his defense. Our experts in philosophical criticism, instead, whenever they are confronted with some dubious point, are wont to say, "Give me some time to think it over!" (15)

In his *Autobiography*, Vico praises his own versatile eloquence and stresses the practical importance of rhetorical dexterity as he recounts the delivery of his fourth commencement oration at the university, in 1704:

> Vico had delivered half of this discourse when Don Feliz Lanzina Ulloa, president of the Sacred Council and the Cato of the Spanish ministers, joined the audience. In his honor Vico with great presence of mind gave a new and briefer turn to what had gone before and united it with what he had left to say. (142)

At the same time that Vico is pressing the importance of ready eloquence to his students preparing for careers in politics and law, he is proposing that eloquence is more a bonus than a goal for the philosopher-in-life; eloquence is the occasional and useful by-product of the mature philosophic imagination (here Vico follows Cicero, as Ernesto Grassi has argued). Vico makes the student's "specifically philosophic faculty" to invent relationships prerequisite to engaging oratory: "It is this capacity which constitutes the source and principle of all ingenious, acute, and brilliant forms of expression" (24).

Vico's advocacy of rhetoric as the exercise of philosophic imagination is "classical" in its echoes of Plato, Aristotle, and Cicero and "modern" in its relevance to the prevailing association of literacy with certainty, correctness, and efficiency; his work continues the tradition that calls into question an emphatically pragmatic and utilitarian view of rhetoric and writing. Vico would have us reconsider a curriculum in which rhetoric is purely instrumental, instead of exploratory; a curriculum in which invention is forgotten. And I must emphasize that invention does not mean, for Vico, *preliminary* exploration; it is, rather, the continual synthesis of knowledge and experience in a context that is always new, mindful that "nature and life are full of incertitude" (15):

> Today, having made the discovery of a single truth, we proceed to draw from it a whole series of inferences concerning the phenomena of Nature. But symptoms and judgments, drawn from long-continued observation, are merely probable approximations to truth. Francis Bacon charges that the followers of Galen, who employ the syllogism, reach wrong conclusions concerning the causes of disease. Like Bacon, I would maintain that the moderns are led astray by their fondness for that strictly deductive form of reasoning which the Greeks called *sorites* [syllogistic reasoning]. The person who uses the syllogism brings no new element, since the conclusion is already implied in the initial proposition or assumption: analogously, those who employ the sorites merely unfold the secondary truth which lies within the primary statement. Now illnesses are always new and different, and no two sick people are ever alike. Nor am I, at the present moment, the same individual I was but a minute ago while talking of the sick: countless life-instants have already passed by, numberless motions have already taken place, by which I am continuously pushed in the direction of my last day. Thus, since every genus (and every true genus contains a whole series of particular cases) contains an exceedingly great number of specific diseases, and these diseases cannot all be categorized under a single general class name, it is impossible for us to attain truth in this sphere, either through the syllogism, since its major premise consists of a general notion (and particular instances cannot be subsumed under a general notion), or through the strictly deductive procedure of the sorites. (*Study Methods* 32)

Reasoning that presumes stable and linear causal relationships denies that the circumstances of each moment are always "new and different." Because changing circumstances alter meaning and truth, the philosopher-in-life invents new "causes" incessantly.

Hume, *Enquiry Concerning Human Understanding*

David Hume, a student of Montaigne (Mossner 79) and the most extreme philosophic skeptic in eighteenth-century Britain, shares with Vico a preoccupation with how associational thinking creates knowledge and discourse and the recognition that "all is uncertain and . . . our judgment is not in *any* thing possessed of *any* measure of truth and falsehood" (Hume, *Treatise on Human Nature* 183). While his friends Hugh Blair and George Campbell remain consequential voices in rhetorical theory and pedagogy, it is Hume who proffers the most radical challenge to their legacy. As his *Enquiry Concerning Human Understanding* evolves, with stronger emphasis on the free-associative nature of the mind, Hume sets aside the virtues of unity, perspicuity, and closure that British rhetoric and belles-lettres exhorted.

Although Hume belongs in the empiricist tradition with both Locke and Berkeley, he stands apart as "one of the greatest skeptics in the history of philosophy" (Popkin 103). Locke stressed the "sensitive" knowledge of finite things, but also believed in "intuitive" knowledge (of one's own existence) and "demonstrative" knowledge (of God). Whereas Locke believed that sensible things do exist, Berkeley argued that they do not; all that exists is our perception, and that is caused by God. Hume refuted both Locke and Berkeley, holding that the only knowledge available comes from what we directly observe; he denied both intuitive knowledge and divine inspiration. In effect, Hume erased all absolutes from previous empiricist philosophy (Bennett *passim*).

The *Enquiry Concerning Human Understanding* differs from its more abstruse predecessor, *Treatise on Human Nature*, "more in emphasis than in argument" (Ayer 6) and represents significant revisions in Hume's philosophic thought, including a retraction of conventional belletristic precepts. *Human Understanding* tries to explain how we know the world and begins by distinguishing impressions and ideas:

> By the term *impression*, then, I mean all our more lively perceptions, when we hear, or see, or feel, or love, or hate, or desire, or will. And impressions are distinguished from ideas, which are the less lively perceptions, of which we are conscious, when we reflect on any of those sensations or movements above mentioned. (*Philosophical Works* IV, 14)

Because ideas are alway occasioned by impressions, they will vary from individual to individual, from culture to culture, from age to age: "A Laplander or Negro has no notion of the relish of wind . . . a man of mild manner can form no idea of inveterate revenge or cruelty; nor can a selfish heart conceive the heights of friendship or generosity" (IV, 15). Hume's examples may seem presumptuous and overly simplified, but the point stands that experience is raw material and that any idea not rooted in experience must be rejected as invalid. Hume would put ideas, especially philosophical ones, to an empirical test. His famous conclusion to *Human Understanding* reaffirms the importance of empirical verification:

> If we take in our hand any volume, of divinity or school metaphysics, for instance, let us ask, *Does it contain any abstract reasoning concerning quantity or number?* No. *Does it contain any experimental reasoning concerning matter of fact and existence?* No. Commit it then to the flames: for it can contain nothing but sophistry and illusion. (IV, 135)

Any philosophy, then, must connect itself with the tangible world. With Montaigne and Vico, Hume puts the philosopher in life and stresses throughout the *Treatise* and the *Enquiry* that the matters of fact verifying the philosophic speculation are always contingent and transitory.

In section III, "Of the Association of Ideas," Hume briefly presents the "principle of connection between the different thoughts or ideas in the mind." Ideas are connected by "resemblance, contiguity in time or place, and cause or effect." This section, as revised for his final edition, includes only three paragraphs and avoids defining these key terms in any detail (IV, 17–19). This change drastically reduces the attention that associationism had received in the *Treatise* and the earlier editions of *Human Understanding*. A further summary of the important principles in *Human Understanding* supplies a context for examining the changes in this section, changes which are crucial to the relationship between Hume's philosophy and rhetorical theory.

Section IV addresses Hume's "Sceptical Doubts Concerning the Operation of the Understanding." Here he states that "All the objects of human reason or enquiry may naturally be divided into two kinds, to wit, *relations of ideas* and *matters of fact*" (IV, 20). Relations of ideas are constructions of the mind which are not based on experience, for instance, "the sciences of geometry, algebra, and arithmetic." Such demonstrative propositions as a geometric theorem are not contestable, according to Hume, but matters of fact are. Matters of fact are conclusions based on experience, "founded on the relation of cause and effect," and since the perception of cause-effect relationships varies as experience varies, a matter of fact from one perspective may not hold true from another. As Hume states about matters of fact in his conclusion to *Human Understanding*, "Whatever *is*, may *not be*" (IV, 134).

That the world is full of diverse and contradictory ideas attests to the power of different experiences to produce different cause-effect relationships. And importantly, this diversity "proceeds entirely from the undeterminate meaning of words" (IV, 134). A statement such as "the square of the hypotenuse is equal to the squares of the other two sides" is incontestable because the meaning of the terms is established and invariable. However, the proposition, "where there is no property, there can be no injustice" is contestable precisely because the terms "property" and "injustice" do not have determinate, invariable meanings. Hume makes this point in the conclusion of *Human Understanding* in order to warn against the "pretended syllogistic reasonings" which may be found in all branches of learning and to encourage philosophers to test their ideas empirically, in the full knowledge that because experience is relative, so are the ideas it engenders.

That people do dispute ideas, especially those concerning ultimate questions of human nature, attests to the inherent ambiguity of language. When "a controversy has been long kept on

foot, and remains still undecided, we may presume that there is
some ambiguity in the expression, and that the disputants affix
different ideas to the terms employed in the controversy." Thus
Hume begins section VIII of *Human Understanding*, which pulls
together the major tenets of his philosophy to address the concepts
of "liberty and necessity," concepts scrutinized repeatedly by the
philosopher's predecessors. Recognizing that "the whole controversy has hitherto turned merely upon words," Hume promises
to present a "just and precise idea" and thereby, we presume,
resolve the controversy. Instead, he calls into question the value
of any "just and precise idea."

Returning to his assertions about cause and effect, Hume
once again makes the point that we infer causality from our perception of "customary conjunctions," "where similar objects are
constantly conjoined, and the mind is determined by custom to
infer one from the appearance of the other." Because events are
experientially but not necessarily connected, because lack of property does not necessarily coincide with injustice, causation is a
convenient illusion:

> We must not . . . expect that . . . uniformity of human actions
> should be carried to such a length, as that all men, in the
> same circumstances, will always act precisely in the same
> manner, without making any allowance for diversity of char-
> acters, prejudices, and opinions. Such a uniformity in every
> particular is found in no part of nature. On the contrary,
> from observing the variety of conduct in different men, we
> are enabled to form a greater variety of maxims, which still
> suppose a degree of uniformity and regularity. (IV, 70)

The "degree of uniformity and regularity" which allows us to speak
in terms like "cause and effect" informs what Hume calls *custom*:

> Custom, then, is the great guide of human life. It is that
> principle alone which renders our experience useful to us
> and makes us expect, for the future, a similar train of events
> with those which have appeared in the past. (IV, 39)

Hume recognizes the power of the mind to create new matters of fact, but admits that custom both restricts this power and allows us to act on our day-to-day concerns. As he states in section V, there is "nothing more free than the imagination of man." As a check to the license of imagination, common experiences and shared assumptions ensure our construction of "customary" connections between past and future, this and that; otherwise "we should never know how to adjust means to ends, or to employ our natural powers in the production of any effect" (IV, 39).

Although Hume values custom as a force which helps us to link ideas and communicate with each other, his philosophy largely comprises a warning that we not confuse reality with custom. In reality, events are distinct, language is ambiguous, and the mind has unlimited powers of creation. By behaving as if necessary connections do operate in the world, as if matters of fact represent truth, we keep ourselves from inquiring into matters taken for granted, from considering the possibility that "Whatever *is*, may not *be*."

Human Understanding, like Vico's *Study Methods*, explains a mental process in which experience and custom combine to produce contingent truths. Hume's primary concern is to explain those principles of connection that convert distinct ideas into a series that seems coherent. By pointing up the free-floating power of the mind, Hume means to temper our certainty that any chain of events is immutable; the mind can always "feign a train of events, with all the appearance of reality, ascribe to them a particular time and place, conceive them as existent, and point them out to itself with every circumstance . . . which it believes with the greatest certainty" (IV, 41). Significantly, Hume states that art is the province most appropriate for depicting the processes of human nature and understanding; early in *Human Understanding* he describes various methods for presenting "pictures of human life" and concludes:

> An artist must be better qualified to succeed in this undertaking, who, besides a delicate taste and a quick apprehension, possesses an accurate knowledge of the internal fabric, the operations of the understanding, the workings of the passions,

and the various species of sentiment which discriminate vice and virtue. (IV, 7)

This statement elevates comprehensive philosophy to a species of art, and also implies the responsibility of the artist to depict human psychology accurately; as Hume continues, "Accuracy is, in every case, advantageous to beauty."

To summarize: Our thinking has form insofar as we link ideas according to both custom and imagination. Certain trains of thought, reinforced by experience and custom, produce matters of fact; but each mind has the power, and the responsibility, to reconsider matters taken for granted and recombine ideas in fresh ways. Art has the power and the responsibility to portray human psychology accurately and beautifully. Given this construction of Hume's philosophy, we would expect him to approve such art as represents the tension between certainty and uncertainty, between custom and imagination, that informs the human "internal fabric."

Locating the explication of philosophic skepticism in art, Hume prompts consideration of the principles and practice of literary discourse which were congruent with the principles and practice of rhetoric. Rhetoric and belles-lettres had been inseparable subjects, informed by the same critical and pedagogical lexicon, since the Middle Ages; as an extended discussion of Hugh Blair's *Lectures on Rhetoric and Belles-Lettres* in the next chapter will show, effective rhetoric and literary art share certain prescribed values, not the least of which is a clear and precise relationship between parts and whole. The value of coherence reflects the value of perspicuity, and both a coherent narrative and perspicuous style appeal to audience psychology. The writer who creates a text of "circumlocutions" is defined as a bad writer because he disrespects traditional rules. Blair's criteria for judging both fiction and nonfiction represent the conventional Enlightenment view of rhetoric and literature; as such, his *Lectures* focus upon regimented style and form and bypass the importance of invention and imagination, of writing as a way of creating rather than merely managing ideas.

In *Human Understanding*, Hume excises the portion of section III that presents principles of literary form inconsistent with his philosophy, which imply that discourse is formally inflexible and rule-generated; this change, which I will detail below, is part of a

final revision that incorporated Hume's doubt about his own categorical statements on human intellection. The version of section
III, "Of the Association of Ideas," which represents Hume's final
revision and is reprinted in all editions after 1777, is reduced to
three paragraphs sketching the principles of resemblance, contiguity, and cause and effect. We presume that this version constitutes the "final draft" of Hume's philosophy, especially because in
the "Advertisement" to the 1777 edition, Hume wrote: "The
author desires that the following pieces may alone be regarded as
containing his philosophical sentiments and principles" (III, 38).

The chapter "Of the Connection or Association of Ideas"
had appeared in the 1739 *Treatise*, and "Of the Association of
Ideas" had appeared in the 1748 *Philosophical Essays Concerning Human
Understanding*. In both the *Treatise* and the *Abstract of the Treatise on
Human Nature* (published anonymously in 1740), Hume celebrated
his principles of association as a great discovery: " 'Twill be easy
to conceive of what vast consequence these principles must be in
the science of human nature" (Cohen 547). By the time he writes
the 1748 *Human Understanding*, Hume has removed explicit statements of praise for the principles of association and seems somewhat uncertain about whether such principles do exclusively account
for the association of ideas. In 1740 the tone of his assertions is
objective and insistent:

> The qualities, from which this association arises, and by which
> the mind is after this manner conveyed from one idea to
> another, are three, *viz.* resemblance, contiguity in time or
> place, and cause and effect.
>
> I believe it will not be very necessary to prove that these
> qualities produce an association among ideas and upon the
> appearance of one idea naturally introduce another. (I, 319)

By 1748 there is less insistence upon the unimpeachable rightness
of his discovery, and a greater willingness to present his findings
as a personal observation:

> *To me*, there *appear to be* only three principles of connection
> among ideas, namely, resemblance, contiguity in time or place,
> and cause and effect. . . . But that this enumeration is com-

plete, and that there are no other principles of association except these, *may be difficult to prove* to the satisfaction of the reader, or even to a man's own satisfaction. (IV, 17, my emphasis)

Hume then states that "more assurance" of the centrality of these principles comes from the repeated examination and enumeration of illustrative instances, but omits the same exhaustive illustrations that characterize the *Treatise* chapters, "Of Relations," "Of Modes and Substances," "Of Abstract Ideas," and the long discussion of space and time. Both the changed tone and the omissions support one well-known fact, that Hume did want to present his ideas more directly and briefly in *Human Understanding* to gain the audience he had not found with the *Treatise*. Also apparent, however, are the qualifications that question Hume's certainty; the shift from writing "The qualities . . . are three" to writing "To me, there appear to be only three principles" signals Hume's evolving belief that matters of fact, including his own assertions, are contingent and relative.

We have these indications that, from 1740 to 1748, Hume ambiguated his stance. However, the 1748 edition of "Of the Association of Ideas" includes a long, dogmatic recital of formulary principles of discourse (IV, 19–23n): sixteen substantial paragraphs surveying the contemporary rules for literary unity, which Hume finds congenial to his principles of association as they affect the imagination. He first emphasizes the importance of a *plan* to a literary work: "A production without a design would resemble more the ravings of a madman than the sober efforts of genius and learning"; this rule "admits of no exception" and the presence of a design allows that "the events or actions, which the writer relates, must be connected together."

After mentioning different species of composition that should exemplify different kinds of unity, Hume focuses the body of his remarks on epic poetry. He first warns against interrupting the narration for too long a time, with "minute circumstances" and "remote causes"; in the face of such interruption, the reader's attention "must flag long before the period of narration." Poets are also warned against introducing "an actor who has no connection, or but a small one, with the principal personages of the fable"; to

be "entertained on the sudden with a new action and new personages" is a "breach in the connection of ideas." In any narrative
poem, "the first proposition of design confines the author to one
subject; and any digressions of this nature would, at first view, be
rejected as absurd and monstrous."

Hume presents each of these constraints as "operations of
the human mind [that] depend on the connection or association
of ideas which is here explained." Although this 1748 edition of
Human Understanding may have been less absolute about the exclusive importance of resemblance, contiguity, and cause and effect,
Hume offers no uncertainty or qualification as he mimics the
codified literary principles of the age (which remain in vogue—
via Blair's *Lectures* and similar texts—well into our century). Hume's
unyielding stance is at odds with his emphasis elsewhere upon the
especially artistic power to produce other than customary associations. In 1748, Hume is arguing in favor of adjusting literary
form to suit readers whose expectations are rooted in traditional
assumptions about unity. Literature, he believes, should be gov-
erned in an obvious way by resemblance, contiguity, and cause
and effect. Such a requirement does not allow for the possibility
of literary innovations which result from the "mixing, compounding, separating, and dividing of ideas" that Hume approves repeatedly in his work.

Hume's removal of the sixteen paragraphs on epic poetry for
the 1777 edition of *Human Understanding* suggests his awareness of
this contradiction and indicates his feeling that both thinking and
writing could follow the free play of the mind. Further evidence
that Hume was amenable to a more "open" discourse by 1777
comes from a letter he sent to William Strahan in 1773:

> The best Book, that has been writ by any Englishman these
> thirty years (for Dr Franklyn is an American) is Tristram
> Shandy, bad as it is. A remark which may astonish you, but
> which you will find true upon Reflection. (Grieg, *Letters* II,
> 269)

Hume had met Sterne in 1764, and they became friends. *Tristram
Shandy* was published at intervals between 1760 and 1767. Hume's
great liking for a book that flouts narrative unity is much more

consistent with his overall philosophy than his earlier insistence upon rigid adherence to rules of arrangement; and the inconsistencies and changes over the life of his work—whatever conclusions they allow—manifest the energy of uncertainty. With his significant excision of compositional principles, Hume posits *Human Understanding* as an implicit philosophy of rhetoric and belles-lettres, a philosophy that emphasizes the potential of the internal fabric of the mind for creative expression.

CHAPTER THREE

The Psychology
of Reading:
Blair, Byron,
DeQuincey

While Montaigne, Vico, and Hume resisted a positivistic
epistemology that exalted knowledge-as-information, that epistemology continued to inform mainstream rhetoric and the teaching
of writing through the nineteenth century. Prescriptions for fine
writing—with their attendant critique of literary style—advanced
an influential theory of reading as well. The most influential exponent
of this theory was Hugh Blair, whose 1783 *Lectures on Rhetoric and
Belles-Lettres* was the text for generations of students. The most
radical and controversial nineteenth-century challenges to Blair's
"plain style" prescriptions were Byron's *Don Juan* and DeQuincey's
essays on rhetoric and style. Byron's poem locates the social,
political, and literary villainies of the early nineteenth century in
the stolid use of language; for this reason, *Don Juan* constitutes an
"anti-rhetoric" to Blair's *Lectures* and the attitudes and practices
they enfranchise.

From Byron's day to this, a repeated issue in the criticism
of *Don Juan* has been the poet's flamboyant refusal to respect consistency and coherence, and his embodiment of that refusal in a
narrator whose mind seems to wander through a series of incongruous topics. The poet's British contemporaries seized upon the

poem's moral incongruities and criticized Byron's oscillations between an ennobling view of human nature and a degrading one.
Leigh Hunt's response to *Don Juan* is representative: Hunt complains
that he is "surprised and moved by a touching piece of human
nature, and again startled and pained by a sudden transition from
loveliness and grandeur to ridicule or the mock heroic" (*Examiner*,
October 31, 1819, 700).[1] As Keith Walker has shown in his extensive study of Byron's readers, comments such as Hunt's define
an audience not only offended by the poet's immorality, but also
confused and angered by the digressive narrative mode in general
(Walker, *passim*); letters and reviews of the time are full of attacks
against "the puzzling want of connection" in *Don Juan* and claims
that Byron's Muse has become "a mixture of metaphysical scraps"
(*British Critic* 20, November 1823, 524–30). Counterposing the free
play of *Don Juan* to Blair's *Lectures*, we see that readers raised on
Blair would find *Don Juan* shapeless and offensive.

Blair, *Lectures on Rhetoric and Belles-Lettres*

Hugh Blair began delivering his lectures in 1759 at the University of Edinburgh. In 1762 he was officially appointed Regius
Professor of Rhetoric and Belles-Lettres. He retired in 1783 and
immediately published the *Lectures*; so great was Blair's reputation
that publisher William Strahan paid the remarkable sum of £1500
for the text and ordered a large first printing. By the end of the
eighteenth century, "half the educated English-speaking world was
reading Blair"; his lectures had become part of the school curriculum throughout both England and America (Charvat 49). Between
1783 and 1873, sixty-two English and American editions were
published, in addition to fifty-one abridged editions. At least 130
editions have been recorded to date, and there have been a number
of translations in Italian, Spanish, French, and Russian. Blair's work
enjoyed a wider sale and greater public approbation in the late
eighteenth and nineteenth centuries than did any other treatment
of rhetoric and literature. It is highly unlikely that any literate
Englishman in Byron's time was not familiar with and influenced
by Blair's work.

Blair intended to teach college students the principles of expository writing and speaking and to guide their appreciation of good literature. Throughout the forty-seven lectures, he stresses the importance of a thorough knowledge of one's subject. He makes it clear that a stylistically deficient text reflects a writer who doesn't know what he thinks; anything less than a clear conception of one's subject guarantees defective work, "so close is the connection between thoughts and the words in which they are clothed" (I, 7). Blair justifies his emphasis on clarity and coherence by pointing out that such qualities coincide with both an always-prevalent audience psychology and a universal tendency in language toward greater refinement. He aligns taste with that pleasure "which arises from the plan or story being well-conducted, and all the parts joined together with due connection" (I, 21). He argues that the value of unity stems from an observation so common since Antiquity that it must signal an "internal sense" in humankind, that sense of "superior pleasure which we receive from the relation of an action which is one and entire, beyond what we receive from the relation of scattered and unconnected facts" (I, 37). In sum, Blair equates taste with the delighted perception of wholeness and posits such delight as a psychological given. He makes this remark by way of connecting taste with literary criticism and concludes that good criticism approves unity above all else.

Blair's doctrine of perspicuity further connects least effort on the reader's part with admirable writing. In Lecture 10 we are told that style discloses the writer's manner of thinking and that perspicuous style is preferred because it reflects an unwavering point of view on the part of the author. Once again we are reminded that certainty is a sign of intellectual strength and that any writer who provides multiple perspectives disables his reader's understanding:

> If, by unnecessarily varying the expression, you shift the point of view, and make me see sometimes the object itself, and sometimes another thing that is connected with it; you thereby oblige me to look on several objects at once, and I lose sight of the principal. (I, 190)

By remarking that the virtue of an unwavering point of view "may be deduced from the nature of the human mind," Blair emphasizes the psychological reality of his tenets.

These rhetorical principles become, in the course of the *Lectures*, inseparable from a theory of literature and language in general. When Blair presents a list of words whose meanings are commonly confused by students (I, 200), he reinforces his belief that no two words have the same meaning and that every single word has only one meaning. This becomes most evident in Lectures 6 and 7 on the origins of language. To begin Lecture 6, "On the Rise and Progress of Language," Blair admits that the connection between words and ideas is arbitrary and conventional, "owing to the agreement of men among themselves." This fact explains for him why modern language is necessarily "better" than the language of earlier ages: as society becomes more polished, refined, and unified, so does language:

> In the infancy of all societies, men are much under the dominion of imagination and passion. They live scattered and dispersed; they are unacquainted with the course of things; they are, every day, meeting with new and strange objects. Fear and surprise, wonder and astonishment, are their most frequent passions. Their language will necessarily partake of this character of their minds. They will be prone to exaggeration and hyperbole. They will be given to describe every thing with the strongest colors and most vehement expressions; infinitely more than men living in the advanced and cultivated periods of society, when their imagination is more chastened, their passions more tamed, and a wider experience has rendered the objects of life more familiar to them. (I, 113)

The progress of society corresponds with the progress of language and with the "progress" of more imaginative expression to less imaginative expression. Further, the advancement of language involves a reduction of figurative expressions because we have available a larger lexicon of precise words obviating the primitive necessity for "circumlocutions." Through history then, understanding has gained ground on imagination, and "language is become, in modern times, more correct, indeed, and accurate" (I, 24). Not to respect lexical precision is to remain uncivilized; this seems to be Blair's message. And with this message, he echoes beliefs prevalent at least since the later seventeenth century, when Thomas Sprat called for a return to "pure" language, exhorting the members of the Royal Society to "reject all amplifications, digressions, and swellings of style; to return back to the primitive purity, and shortness, when men delivered so many *things*, in an almost equal number of *words*" (Sprat 113).

Relative to *Don Juan*, Blair seems quite right to associate unclear style and arrangement with ideas not fully conceived. As Byron says in Canto IX, "So I ramble, now and then narrating, now pondering." Despite his repeated "apologies" for digressing, the poet believes that disconnectedness is a mode appropriate to a genuine search for new lines of thought, and for the replication of the real disconnectedness of "things existent." Blair not only exalts unity, but also makes inconclusiveness a major defect, a symptom of intellectual weakness rather than courage; thus he justifies any discomfort arising from a text such as *Don Juan*, in which "streams of contradiction" continually present us with several objects at once. Byron's goal is never the perspicuous language of precise narration, because the doctrine of perspicuity ignores the multifarious context which affects meaning and which becomes more complex as human knowledge and civilization expand. When Byron at one point in *Don Juan* places Blair among "the highest reachers/Of eloquence in piety and prose" (II, 165), and elsewhere says, "I mean to be perspicuous" (XI, 67), his deliberate irony seems unquestionable.

Byron, *Don Juan*

Don Juan invokes Montaigne and Hume, not Blair. Writing to John Kinnaird about *Don Juan* in 1823, Byron says, "You must not mind occasional rambling. I mean it for a poetical T[ristram Shandy]—or Montaigne's Essays with a story for a hinge" (Marchand, *Letters* X, 40). Byron's letters show further that he had read Hume before leaving Cambridge and that he was reading parts of *Human Understanding* while writing *Don Juan* (*Letters* I, 14–15; II,

97; IV, 161; VI, 59). Stanzas 29–39 in Canto V typify the way in which Byron exploits the associative power of imagination, by representing a broad range of subjects within a short space:

At last they settled into simple grumbling,
　　　And pulling out reluctant purses, and
Turning each piece of silver o'er, and tumbling
　　　Some down, and weighing others in their hand,
And by mistake sequins with *paras* jumbling,
　　　Until the sum was accurately scanned,
And then the merchant giving change, and signing
Receipts in full, began to think of dining.

I wonder if his appetite was good?
　　　Or, if it were, if also his digestion?
Methinks at meals some odd thoughts might intrude,
　　　And Conscience ask a curious sort of question,
About the right divine how far we should
　　　Sell flesh and blood. When dinner has oppressed one,
I think it is perhaps the gloomiest hour
Which turns up out of the sad twenty-four.

Voltaire says "No": he tells you that Candide
　　　Found life most tolerable after meals;
He's wrong—unless man were a pig, indeed,
　　　Repletion rather adds to what he feels,
Unless he's drunk, and then no doubt he's freed
　　　From his own brain's oppression while it reels.
Of food I think with Philip's son or rather
Ammon's (ill pleased with one world and one father);

I think with Alexander, that the act
　　　Of eating, with another act or two,
Makes us feel our mortality in fact
　　　Redoubled; when a roast and a ragout,
And fish, and soup, by some side dishes backed,
　　　Can give us either pain or pleasure, who
Would pique himself on intellects, whose use
Depends so much upon the gastric juice?

The other evening ('t was on Friday last)—
  This is a fact, and no poetic fable—
Just as my greatcoat was about me cast,
  My hat and gloves still lying on the table,
I heard a shot—'t was eight o'clock scarce past—
  And, running out as fast as I was able,
I found the military commandant
Stretched in the street, and able scarce to pant.

Poor fellow! for some reason, surely bad,
  They had slain him with five slugs; and left him there
To perish on the pavement; so I had
  Him borne into the house and up the stair,
And stripped, and looked to,—But why should I add
  More circumstances? vain was every care;
The man was gone—in some Italian quarrel
Killed by five bullets from an old gun-barrel.

I gazed upon him, for I knew him well;
  And though I have seen many corpses, never
Saw one, whom such an accident befell,
  So calm; though pierced through stomach, heart, and liver,
He seemed to sleep,—for you could scarcely tell
  (As he bled inwardly, no hideous river
Of gore divulged the cause) that he was dead:
So as I gazed on him, I thought or said—

"Can this be Death? then what is Life or Death?
  Speak!" but he spoke not: "wake!" but still he slept:—
"But yesterday and who had mightier breath?
  A thousand warriors by his word were kept
In awe: he said, as the Centurion saith,
  'Go,' and he goeth; 'come,' and forth he stepped.
The trump and bugle till he spake were dumb—
And now nought left him but the muffled drum."

And they who waited once and worshipped—they
  With their rough faces thronged about the bed
To gaze once more on the commanding clay
  Which for the last, though not the first, time bled;

And such an end! that he who many a day
    Had faced Napoleon's foes until they fled,—
The foremost in the charge or in the sally,
Should now be butchered in a civic alley.

The scars of his old wounds were near his new,
    Those honorable scars which brought him fame;
And horrid was the contrast to the view—
    But let me quit the theme; as such things claim
Perhaps even more attention than is due
    From me: I gazed (as oft I have gazed the same)
To try if I could wrench aught out of Death
Which should confirm, or shake, or make a faith;

But it was all a mystery. Here we are,
    And there we go:—but *where*? five bits of lead,
Or three, or two, or one, send very far!
    And is this blood, then formed but to be shed?
Can every element our elements mar?
    And Air—Earth—Water—Fire live—and we dead?
We, whose minds comprehend all things? No more;
But let us to the story as before.

The excerpt begins with the conclusion of a slave auction at which
Don Juan has been purchased; Baba, the purchaser, has just finished
haggling with the merchant over price, and the merchant begins
to anticipate his evening meal. The narrator suddenly interposes:
"I wonder if his appetite was good?" and thus commences a four-
stanza speculation about the relationship between selling flesh, eating
flesh, and existing as mortal flesh ourselves. Stanza 33 abruptly turns
to the murder of a military commandant which has occurred in
the narrator's (indeed Byron's) own experience. As the commandant succumbs, the narrator wonders, "Can this be Death? then
what is Life or Death?" and pursues inconclusively the mystery of
human mortality. Such ruminations end as suddenly as they had
begun, with "No more;/But let us to the story as before." While
reading these stanzas, we are alternately pulled out of and back
into the world of the poem without the aid of any explicit transitions. But the accessibility of this section to a summary, even a

superficial one, suggests that a perceptible continuity, however implicit and subtle, does operate in the poem.

Metonymy is one term for expressing the continuity in *Don Juan*. This is not apparent until we reconsider metonymy as not merely the emblematic substitution of one term for another, but rather as the process that links imaginative worlds in subtle ways. Such is the understanding of Roman Jakobson and Kenneth Burke; both view metonymy as a device of "poetic realism" and variegated form. For Jakobson, metonymy allows the poet to digress "from the plot to the atmosphere and from the characters to the setting in space and time" (1114). For Burke, metonymy is the process that links the "corporeal, visible, tangible" world by analogy with the "incorporeal, invisible, intangible" (*Grammar* 506). In stanzas 29–39, we are moved from the specific, visible world of the slave auction and its hungry merchant through more general, less visible considerations of appetite, digestion, and slavery, into purely intellectual speculation about mortality, and back to a new visible world dominated by a death. The remaining stanzas continue to bridge the visible and invisible worlds, extending from a description of the corpse to the memory of his past deeds, to another attempt to explain death in general, an attempt which ends with a quick reversion to what Burke would call "the original corporeal reference," that is, the story of the adventures of Don Juan. Thus Byron inserts worlds within worlds, the tangible world within the intangible within the tangible, and so forth. The poem spins itself out in this way, without dwelling with a consistent point of view in any stretch of discourse.

We might want to propose now that Byron typically creates a chain of metonymic equivalences to attest to both the unity of an apparently jumbled poem and the transcendental unity of an apparently jumbled world. Notice that the subtle association between the visible world of a slave trader's dinner and the invisible world of death helps us to construct a view of mortality that both unifies and transcends the sum of its parts. Selling flesh becomes a symbolic enactment of the way death finally devours man. With this in mind, we are no longer sure where the "real" world ends and the "imagined" world begins, and we do sense a wholeness informing the world of the poem, a wholeness which implies a real world with essence and purpose (in this case a diabolical essence and a destructive purpose).

But we must be careful about confusing coherence with some larger wholeness or purposefulness. Byron's use of metonymy to achieve coherence is a trick, albeit a good and valuable one, and one which we use to trick ourselves all the time. Put another way: The search for unity is one of the consistent elements of reading; conducting that search through *Don Juan* we find repeated metonymic progressions in which death consistently dominates and frustrates human idealism. Therefore, we might want to conclude that, in *Don Juan*, the world *means* death. This is a myopic reading, as limited as accumulating all the narrator's perceptions of beauty to conclude that Byron's world celebrates life. Neither does the poem present a tension between dualisms: death and life, good and evil, and so forth. Byron's metonymy does not posit any expressible worldview, but demonstrates stylistically what Byron insists upon in other ways throughout the poem, that the *word* relationships that we construct to make sense of *Don Juan* are not to be generalized into *world* relationships. To identify the figurative coherence of the poem with a comprehensible real world, one needs to believe that the phrase, "We, who comprehend all things" in stanza 39, is meant to state a truth to which Byron subscribes, that it is possible for humans to *progress* toward ultimate knowledge. But the lines that immediately precede that phrase pose a question which denies this possibility, a question that the narrator repeats throughout the poem:

> I gazed (as oft I have gazed the same)
> To try if I could wrench aught out of Death
> Which should confirm, or shake, or make a faith;
>
> But it was all a mystery. Here we are,
>   And there we go:——but *where*?

The perceived relationship between the visible and the invisible world, which I have called metonymic coherence, will not "confirm, or shake, or make a faith" in life or death. That is, although we have in this poem a *progression* of subtly related terms, we have no *progress*—no greater clarity, no greater insight into the mysteries of existence. Consider stanzas 133–34 from Canto I:

> Man's a phenomenon, one knows not what,
>   And wonderful beyond all wondrous measure;
> 'T is a pity though, in this sublime world, that
>   Pleasure's a sin, and sometimes Sin's a pleasure;
> Few mortals know what end they would be at,
>   But whether Glory, Power, or Love, or Treasure,
> The path is through perplexing ways, and when
> The goal is gained, we die, you know—and then—
>
> What then?—I do not know, no more do you—
>   And so good night.—Return we to our story:

Terms like "sublime" and "wonderful beyond all wondrous measure" resonate against "one knows not what," and the path of life ends with the usual Byronic question: "What then?" What then?—words and more words: "Return we to our story." Without the assurance that real progress is somehow achievable through human effort, the narrator returns us to "our" story; by returning to the plot, we can at least *seem* to make progress, we can participate in a world of action without reflection, peopled by characters who appear to "get somewhere."

The distinction between coherence and wholeness or purposefulness is necessary to an accurate appreciation of *Don Juan*. The poem is coherent insofar as it allows us the intellectual pleasure of making connections between clusters of terms and situations which would normally seem to exclude one another. Metonymy is a device that tricks us into continuing to read *Don Juan* by creating figurative coherence that implies some transcendental unity. Simultaneously, the poet tells us that unity is no more than a linguistic construct. However, the very vitality of Byron's medley style shows the value of language for gathering together so many irresolute impulses of being. As he writes in Canto XV:

> He who doubts all things nothing can deny:
>   Truth's fountains may be clear—her streams are muddy,

And cut through such canals of contradiction,
That she must often navigate o'er fiction.

Throughout *Don Juan*, as Byron shifts from topic to topic, we become aware that the fountain of truth is not allied with this or that idea, but rather that the "true" relationship between "things existent" is itself the free play of words and ideas, the very energy which occurs when streams of thought are forced into contradiction. *Don Juan* forms and reforms itself by at once appealing to everything in us that desires closure and celebrating the power of language to go beyond closure into new uncertainty and new adventure.

Byron's contemporaries saw the poem as a collection of unambiguous information, responding with the opacity of a Phaedrus, and the propriety of Blair. In the December 1821 *British Review*, William Roberts said of *Don Juan*, "We can only review the work as Englishmen and Christians" (246). Thus he defined the critical parameters present in virtually every contemporary review of Byron's poem. The question that greeted each new set of cantos concerned the extent to which *Don Juan* was aligned with English morality, politics, and poetics. And the discontinuous form of the poem represented for readers opportunity to divide *Don Juan* into extracts which they evaluated, respectively, as moral maxims, political maxims, or "poetical" events.[2] The issue of whether the experimental form of this poem represents some imaginative integrity remained largely unexamined while readers carved *Don Juan* into *morceaux* of fictional adventure or liberal propaganda.

By continuing the exclusion of uncertainty, ambiguity, and intellectual play from acceptable discourse, Byron's readers embody a "psychology of information" rather than a "psychology of form," and represent the centuries-long appeal of packaged knowledge to which this study offers counterstatements. The two psychologies have been proposed by Kenneth Burke in his *Counterstatement* to twentieth-century scientism. For Burke, "the hypertrophy of the psychology of information is accompanied by the corresponding atrophy in the psychology of form" (29–44). The more readers are interested in information, the less they are interested in form, that is, the orchestration of a discourse that complicates and enlarges the possibilities for meaning. For Burke, the formal complexity of a work is the measure of its "eloquence." And an audience will be less able to consider such eloquence as they become more attentive to propositional content and story as story.

Keeping in mind this initial explanation of the ratio between form and information, we turn to the contemporary reviews of *Don Juan* to further define the tension between "current-traditional" attitudes and the art of wondering. The reviews of the poem remain our only indication of general reader response, and they may be taken as a strong indication. Periodical reviews, especially those representing an array of publications, will reflect generally held sentiments; as Keith Walker concludes in his survey of Byron's audience, "a magazine has to flatter the susceptibilities of its readers if it is to ensure its own survival" (xi). What we do not get from an examination of reviews is much indication of either lower-class or aristocratic attitudes; the magazines of the period attracted a generally middle-class audience. When I refer to Byron's readers, then, I mean the populous middle class schooled on Blair's *Lectures*, represented by nearly seventy reviews of *Don Juan* published between 1818 and 1824.

William Roberts' criticism in the *British Review* epitomizes the widespread response to the morality of *Don Juan*. The *Review* was an Evangelical publication, so one might expect its outrage at Byron's poem. Not many of Byron's readers were Evangelical, but almost all of them were Christian and supported the moral and ethical values espoused by Roberts. His several reviews generally reflect a seriousness shared with other readers, one informed by moral staunchness. His humorlessness typifies the middle-class response to Byron's moral incongruities:

> Whatsoever things are honest, whatsoever things are pure, whatsoever things are lovely, whatsoever things are of good report, are here brought into contrast with their opposites, in order, as it would seem, that by the display of one withered by the blast of infidel art, and of the other blooming in its own atmosphere of voluptuousness, the triumph of iniquity might be complete, even to the perversion of moral and natural feeling. (August 1819, 266–68)

In *Don Juan*, Byron confounds moral absolutes, certainly. Unable to eschew a dualistic moral view, Roberts reads this blurring of customary distinctions as a contest between good and evil, with Byron as the devil's advocate.

Such a view, of *Don Juan* as a moral contest, pervades so much of criticism of the poem. By the time Cantos VI-VIII are published, a writer for the *British Critic* has come to expect that every virtuous instance of the poem signals a vicious one; he suspects that the friendship between Juan and Leila masks "some future attack on virtue and good feeling" (August 1823, 186). The most numerous indications that *Don Juan* was read as a poem of moral oppositions come through repeated conclusions that in Byron's poem, iniquity triumphs. This is Roberts' point, that the act of bringing good into conjunction with evil, without expressing a clear preference for one or the other, implies a preference for evil. John Wilson, writing for *Blackwood's*, calls the Juan-Haidee idyll in Canto II a "true romance," but insists upon reading the final, digressive stanzas of the canto as a denial of this beautiful relationship; these stanzas about the precarious nature of the "chaste connubial state" seem for Wilson to have "polluted" the purity of the romance entirely and ruined beauty by exposing it to "the very suicide of genius" (August 1819, 512–18). The *British Critic* review of stanzas III–V once again notes that the mixture of the "wholesome" with corruption "turns out to be garbage" (September 1821, 253). And the *British Magazine* complains that the beauty of the seraglio description in Canto VI is ruined by the intrusion of "drunken, drivelling, old gentlemen's after-dinner obscenity" (August 1823, 274).

The *Edinburgh Review*, which had devoted so much space to Byron's earlier work, never "officially" reviewed *Don Juan*, but Francis Jeffrey did detail at some length his reasons for dismissing the poem in a review of *Sardanapalus*. He rejects the poem because it seems informed by moral oppositions that portend the victory of indecency. According to Jeffrey, Byron demonstrates "how possible it is to have all fine and noble feelings, or their appearance, for a moment, and yet retain no particle of respect for them— or belief in their intrinsic worth or permanent reality" (February 1822, 449–50).

All Byron's detractors conclude that the medley of moral stances in *Don Juan* is poisonous, that the variegated morality is analogous to "the graceful folds of the adder," that moral skepticism is really moral corruption. And the charge of corruption results not from the unwillingness to recognize that evil and pain exist, but from the presumption that they cannot coexist simultaneously with goodness without destroying it. As William Roberts declares, "the heart [cannot] at the same time lend itself to two opposite emotions" (December 1821, 245–65). In sum, Byron's readers translate incongruous form into definite information (the poet's allegiance to evil). Thus they betoken the predominant Christianity of Byron's time whose dualistic view of human nature resists any blurring of the distinction between virtue and vice.

While the conversion of form into moral information accounts for the condemnation of *Don Juan*, it also accounts for misplaced praise. Stanzas 122–27 of Canto I are admired as a rare instance of beauty by a number of periodicals, notably *Blackwood's,* the *British Critic, Literary Gazette*, and *New Monthly Magazine*. But although the stanzas begin by recognizing the lyrical sweetness of natural beauty, they eventually introduce a definition of sweetness that includes greed and violence:

> 'Tis sweet to hear
> At midnight on the blue and moonlit deep
> The song and oar of Adria's gondolier,
> By distance mellowed, o'er the waters sweep;
> 'Tis sweet to see the evening star appear;
> 'Tis sweet to listen as the night-winds creep
> From leaf to leaf; 'tis sweet to view on high
> The rainbow, based on ocean, span the sky.
>
> 'Tis sweet to hear the watch-dog's honest bark
> Bay deep-mouthed welcome as we draw near home;
> 'Tis sweet to know there is an eye will mark
> Our coming, and look brighter when we come;
> 'Tis sweet to be awakened by the lark,
> Or lulled by falling waters; sweet the hum
> Of bees, the voice of girls, the song of birds,
> The lisp of children, and their earliest words.

Sweet is the vintage, when the showering grapes
    In Bacchanal profusion reel to earth,
Purple and gushing: sweet are our escapes
    From civic revelry to rural mirth;
Sweet to the miser are his glittering heaps,
    Sweet to the father is his first-born's birth,
Sweet is revenge—especially to women—
Pillage to soldiers, prize-money to seamen.

Sweet is a legacy, and passing sweet
    The unexpected death of some old lady,
Or gentleman of seventy years complete,
    Who've made "us youth" wait too—too long already,
For an estate, or cash, or country seat,
    Still breaking, but with stamina so steady,
That all the Israelites are fit to mob its
Next owner for their double-damned post-obits.

'Tis sweet to win, no matter how, one's laurels,
    By blood or ink, 'tis sweet to put an end
To strife; 'tis sometimes sweet to have our quarrels,
    Particularly with a tiresome friend:
Sweet is old wine in bottles, ale in barrels;
    Dear is the helpless creature we defend
Against the world; and dear the schoolboy spot
We ne'er forget, though there we are forgot.

But sweeter still than this, than these, than all
    Is first and passionate Love—it stands alone,
Like Adam's recollection of his fall;
    The Tree of Knowledge has been plucked—all's known
And Life yields nothing further to recall
    Worthy of this ambrosial sin, so shown,
No doubt in fable, as the unforgiven
Fire which Prometheus filched for us from Heaven.

The first twenty lines conform to conceptions (then and now)
of sweetness; however, from the line "Sweet to the miser are his
glittering heaps" sweetness is no longer restricted to innocent
pursuits, but connected with avarice, thievery, bloodshed, drunk-

enness, and death. And even the sweetness of "first and passionate love" is connected with original sin and the fall from grace. Altogether we have another instance of the poet's refusal to stick to a singular view; he joins the term "sweet" to much in life that is usually considered sour, thus committing the sort of offense which readers detected in other parts of the poem, namely, the intermingling of the finer and baser qualities of human life and human nature.

However, only one reviewer seems bothered by the inconsistencies in these stanzas. The writer for the *British Critic* says that stanzas 122 and 123 are "the best stanzas in the poem," but goes on to distinguish them from the rest of this section: "The first two stanzas, and the ideas which they contain are common, and have yet a sweetness, and an elegance in their expression, that gives them an air even of originality. In the third there is a lamentable falling off. . . ." (August 1819, 204). This falling off, he continues, happens because the definitions of "sweet" depart from "custom." John Wilson of *Blackwood's*, who vociferously condemns Byron's pollution of beauty in other places, remarks that all six stanzas are among the most beautiful passages in the poem (August 1819, 515–16). The reviewer for the *Literary Chronicle* also seems to miss the inconsistencies entirely when he summarizes the "'tis sweet" stanzas by saying that "the sweets of early love are powerfully described"; he has missed or ignored the sweets of hate, violence, and greed (July 17, 1819, 129–30). The *Literary Gazette* approvingly mentions "the delighted enumeration of the sweets of life" (July 17, 1819, 450). And the *New Monthly Magazine* applauds the "exquisite beauty" of the first two stanzas and does not at all mention the inconsistencies that follow (August 1819, 75).

Each of these reviewers deplores the poet's mixture of "grave and gay" at other points in the poem and finds that practice immoral. But here Byron's "pollution" of sweetness is ignored in one way or another. The inattentiveness to "negative" sweetness is yet another instance of obscuring the imaginative form of the poem by converting inconsistencies into conventional information and setting aside the possible "perversions" of sweetness that operate outside of its customary definition. As we have seen, one way to explicate the moral shifts in this poem is to turn a series of stances into a moral contest and declare a winner. Another way, in this case, is to ignore any potential moral confusion altogether by seeming not to notice the darker implications of the term.

Only the reviews in the *Examiner*, especially Leigh Hunt's review of Cantos I and II, attempt neither to condemn nor ignore moral incongruity. However, even Hunt feels compelled to fit the poem to a moral law; after summarizing the plot of Canto I, he draws the following conclusion:

> Lord Byron does no more than relate the consequences of certain absurdities. If he speaks slightingly of the ties between a girl and a husband old enough for her father, it is because the ties themselves *are* slight. He does not ridicule the bonds of marriage generally, or where they are formed as they should be: he merely shows the folly and wickedness of setting forms and opinions against nature. (October 31, 1819, 701)

Hunt does not call *Don Juan* immoral and does recognize that the poet is relating a possible and realistic chain of events, rather than advocating corruption. But in his effort to make the poem into a work of "natural" morality, he invents a consistent moral stance where there is none. To say that Byron "does not ridicule the bonds of marriage generally" is wrong; there are no happily married people in Cantos I and II, or anywhere else in the poem. Hunt is using the absence of a categorical statement against marriage to imply the poet's approval of "marriages formed as they should be." And for Hunt this seems merely to mean marriages between young people approximately equal in age. The reviewer seems bent upon extracting a palatable moral proposition from the poem and is unwilling to consider the possibility that the poet is not showing "the folly and wickedness of setting forms and opinions against *nature*" and is instead abjuring the criterion of social *or* natural unity.

Hunt recognizes that much of the moral criticism of *Don Juan* comes from the tendency of readers to define stubbornly and strictly the virtuous and the vicious:

> The fact is, at the bottom of all these questions, that many things are made vicious which are not so by nature; and many things made virtuous which are only so by calling and

agreement: and it is on the horns of this self-created dilemma that society is continually writhing and getting desperate.

Along with Byron, Hunt objects to the tyranny of custom. And yet he too is very uncomfortable with the quick alterations in the poem and sounds very much like all the other reviewers when he objects that the poet "trifles too much with our feelings, and occasionally goes on, turning to ridicule or hopelessness all the fine ideas he has excited, with a recklessness that becomes extremely unpleasant and mortifying."

This review voices the strongest contemporary defense of the moral stances in *Don Juan*, and that defense is based upon a kind of misreading not unlike that of Byron's detractors. For Hunt imposes an intention by deciding that the poem cannot (or should not) be irresolute by design; just as the poet's critics read the poem as a moral contest between virtue and vice, and declare Byron the champion of vice, Hunt portrays a contest between social law and natural law and declares Byron nature's champion. When the digressions become strikingly incongruous, Hunt attributes such form to "recklessness" or to the poet's inability to control "painful and 'thick-coming' recollections." He will find moral unity when he can, and when he cannot he will treat the poetry as a kind of lapse.

After a final burst of moral outrage about the sexual innuendo in Canto VI, most reviewers concentrated upon the political import of *Don Juan*. Byron invited such a focus in the preface to Cantos VI–VII, in which he attacks Castlereagh, Wellington, and the anti-liberal Holy Alliance; admires the radical criminals Waddington and Watson; and compares his own opposition to "the most notorious abuses of the name of God and the mind of man" to the protests of Socrates and Jesus Christ. One could hardly expect readers associated in the preface with "the degraded and hypocritical mass which leavens the present English generation" to admire *Don Juan* as "a versified Aurora Borealis" in the face of this challenge to the national identity.

In general, the reviews exalt "English prejudices, English pursuits, English humor, and the comforts of an English fireside" (*British Critic*, November 1823, 524). *Blackwood's* calls Cantos VI–VIII "heartless, heavy, dull anti-British garbage . . . puffed in the

Examiner ... extolled by Hunt" (July 1823, 88). The *British Critic* argues that Hunt actually wrote a portion of these cantos (August 1823, 178–88). The *Literary Gazette* dismisses VI–VIII as far removed from either public interest or public necessity:

> Nothing is more loathsome to third parties than to be bored with raptures which they never felt, and the debased painting of scenes in which (to say the least) they can have no interest. . . . This country happily does not need saving, in any extreme sense, at present. (July 19, 1823, 451)

The reader here identifies himself with a "third party," to emphasize his non-identification with the poet's audience. A further indication that readers are beginning to disavow their own status as the poet's audience comes in responses to the quotations from Voltaire in the preface, which the *Literary Museum* and *Scots Magazine* read as references only to those with "bad hearts," i.e., thieves. The notion that these later cantos were really about some "third party" and not about the "mass which leavens the present English generation" may have been a factor in the reduced attention to *Don Juan* after Cantos VI–VIII appeared: Cantos VI–VIII were reviewed by fourteen publications, Cantos IX–XI by twelve, Cantos XII–XIV by eight, and Cantos XV–XVI by only three.

Byron's expansive look at the often bitter ironies at play within the national character aroused a categorical denial. The Albion stanzas from Canto X are the most fierce indictment of England in *Don Juan*, an indictment that received an equally fierce response from the poet's contemporaries. Byron describes Juan's first glimpse of the British Isles:

> At length they rose, like a white wall along
>   The blue sea's border; and Don Juan felt—
> What even young strangers feel a little strong
>   At the first sight of Albion's chalky belt—
> A kind of pride that he should be among
>   Those haughty shopkeepers, who sternly dealt
> Their goods and edicts out from pole to pole,
> And made the very billows pay them toll.

I've no great cause to love that spot on earth,
  Which holds what *might have been* the noblest nation;
But though I owe it little but my birth,
  I feel a mixed regret and veneration
For its decaying fame and former worth.
  Seven years (the usual term of transportation)
Of absence lay one's old resentments level,
When a man's country's going to the devil.

Alas! could she but fully, truly, know
  How her great name is now throughout abhorred;
How eager all the Earth is for the blow
  Which shall lay bare her bosom to the sword;
How all the nations deem her their worst foe
  That worse than *worst of foes*, the once adored
False friend, who held out freedom to mankind,
And now would chain them—to the very *mind*;—

Would she be proud, or boast herself the free,
  Who is but the first of slaves? The nations are
In prison,—but the gaoler, what is he?
  No less victim to the bolt and bar.
Is the poor privilege to turn the key
  Upon the captive, Freedom? He's as far
From the enjoyment of the earth and air
Who watches o'er the chain, as they who wear. (65–68)

The "spring of prime" has passed, and this government seeking its own stronger establishment through imperialistic expansion has "butchered half the earth, and bullied t'other."

These stanzas, regarded by contemporaries as the central political statement of the poem, were excerpted often in order to demonstrate "the folly and falsehood of which will be so readily acknowledged by all who read them" (*British Magazine*, September 1823, 297). Reviewers castigate Byron's "lack of patriotism" while they italicize the titles "Lord" and "noble" in order to emphasize that Byron had become unworthy of his station.

What readers favor is a national identity that exemplifies human progress and perfectability. In this connection, the incident at Shooter's Hill is excerpted still more often than the Albion cantos and is certainly the most popular passage in Canto XI. For some readers, this passage counterbalances the want of poetry and want of patriotism in the poet's direct attacks on England. They do not seem to notice that the episode also undercuts sentimental idealism and national pride. Consider the first two stanzas:

> I say, Don Juan, wrapped in contemplation,
> Walked on behind his carriage, o'er the summit,
> And lost in wonder of so great a nation,
> Gave way to 't, since he could not overcome it.
> "And here," he cried, "is Freedom's chosen station;
> Here peals the People's voice nor can entomb it.
> Racks—prisons—inquisitions; Resurrection
> Awaits it, each new meeting or election.

> "Here are chaste wives, pure lives; here people pay
> But what they please; and if that things be dear,
> 'T is only that they love to throw away
> Their case, to show how much they have a-year.
> Here laws are all inviolate—none lay
> Traps for the traveller—every highway's clear—
> Here"—he was interrupted by a knife,
> With—"Damn your eyes! your money or your life!" (9–10)

London at sunset, like Albion's cliffs, calls up patriotic ideas. And those ideas give way to an incongruous reality, in this case footpads who do indeed "damn" Juan's eyes by replacing his glorious observations with an ugly contradiction.

Here and elsewhere the poet scoffs at or curses the sentiment customarily associated with the natural beauties of one's native land. Yet the ironic effect here escapes several adamant representatives of "English prejudices." A reviewer for the *Literary Sketch-book* who dislikes the lack of patriotism in the Albion stanzas declares himself "more pleased" with the Shooter's Hill passage (August 30, 1823, 44). The reader who had noted "the folly and falsehood" of the Albion stanzas in *British Magazine* calls this incident "one of the most poetical and excellent parts" (September 1823, 298). The writer for the *Monthly Review* complains that Byron continues to speak "against . . . the voice of the public" and then prints twelve stanzas of the Shooter's Hill passage as an example of "adventure" (October 1823, 218).

The Shooter's Hill incident is part of the "plot" and not one of the author's direct statements about England, and this fact begins to account for the approval of these readers. The footpad becomes for them what he quite literally is, the villain in an adventure and not the embodiment of a corrupt and greedy England. In the Albion stanzas, the author's ironic juxtaposition may have evoked a judgmental response because the counter to patriotism was explicit and virulent, necessarily calling upon readers to defend their beliefs and condemn falsehood in order to preserve a more perfect image of England. In the Shooter's Hill passage, the juxtaposition of ideal and real is more subtle and centers upon a character quite apart from any notion of a proper Englishman; that the readers miss the subtlety and gloss over the irony speaks for their unquestioning acceptance of a glorious national image. It also speaks for their focus on the literal meaning of fiction.

The responses to the Albion and Shooter's Hill stanzas are both tied to the distinction between form and information. The Albion stanzas are read as political information, an offensive Byronic manifesto, and the Shooter's Hill incident is a story. But the form of both of these passages points up the complexity of what it means to be English. Juxtaposing sentimental praise with angry blame, Byron shows that both are necessary to a full consideration of the national identity and invites our confusion about which view is asserted and which is actually the case.

Certainly Byron's treatment of politics, however various, is never wholly divorced from his particular hate for English conservatism. Insofar as *Don Juan* is published by a radical like Hunt, admires Waddington and Watson, and attacks Castlereagh and Wellington, it espouses a decidedly radical viewpoint. For this reason, Byron's readers were right to accuse the poet of political designs; one must conclude that portions of *Don Juan* are designed to arouse sympathies and antipathies. Byron is political, but he is also more than just a partisan. The contemporary assessment of Byron's partisanship suits the poet's deliberate appeals to political action but tends to overlook the subtle manner in which he enlarges and complicates his own opinion.

Of the thirty-seven reviews that greeted Cantos VI–XIV, only seven expressed any measure of approval, and only those four in the *Literary Examiner* explicitly praise Byron's "liberal sentiments"; the others were generally ambiguous tributes to the poet's "wit." The *Literary Examiner* was inspired by Leigh Hunt and edited by H. L. Hunt, so one would expect it to counterattack the conservative politics in the negative reviews. The remarkable characteristic of H. L. Hunt's notices is their extensive effort to explain the function of form in *Don Juan*; I quote from a review of Cantos VI–VIII:

Looking at *Don Juan* as far as it has gone, it is quite obvious, that having taken up the general conception, Lord Byron has bound himself to no particular series of adventures, but writes on under the influence of his immediate impulses. Every one is aware that there is both loss and gain by this process; that something is lost in unity and consistency of object, and something gained in occasional freshness and spirit. It may be further observed, that, after all, *Don Juan* is not an epic; that we can scarcely conceive an outline more capable of excursion *ad libitum* than the pilotage of a Don Galaor of headlong courage and boundless adventure to the gates of hell. This, however, is a secondary consideration; as we have already hinted, this conspicuous and alarming attribute of Lord Byron is an intuitive perception of the almost mathematical point which marks the confines of vice and virtue, harmlessness and innocence; and a rapid detection of the approximation of extremes, which renders him the Asmodeus or Mephistopheles of poets, a creature which penetrates into your secrets at will. This is startling to every one, but absolutely terrific to the orderly people, who, muffled up to exterior decencies, place well-doing in a mental costume. We never heard an individual express more horror at the first canto of *Don Juan* than a grave merchant, who regularly sent his clerk out of the way to take tea with his wife; or a woman more piously outraged by it than the mistress of the man who married her. These persons felt themselves detected. It is not confounding good and evil to show the slightness of the partitions which divide them; on the contrary, the former may be guarded and secured by a dread of the rapidity of glance which can at once perceive and expose the myriads of lurking avenues by which one can slide into the other. (July 5, 1823, 9)

Other readers, disconcerted by the moral and political content of the poem, angrily dismiss the possibility that it exemplifies any sort of formal integrity. As the poem becomes more digressive in later cantos, their attention to form becomes more brief, pointed, and angry. In this review of Hunt's we have a reader who does not count himself among those "orderly people" who feel threatened by the poem because it unmasks the hypocrisy of the paragon. If Byron's contemporaries missed the subtleties of form in the poem because they were mightily disconcerted by the overt threat to their moral, social, and national identity, we have here someone whose very lack of paranoia coincides with a detailed attention to the function of form. It would seem, in the cases of both H. L. Hunt and Leigh Hunt, that the reduced compulsion to defend oneself against the information in the poem allows a well-developed and eloquent analysis of its experimental form.

Most significant, however, is Hunt's tendency to idealize *Don Juan*. What we get here is greater comfort with the form of the poem, but only because of Hunt's belief that Byron does not confound contraries and does show the "almost mathematical point which marks the confines of vice and virtue," in order to guard and secure virtue from vice. H. L. Hunt, like Leigh Hunt, will not allow the poem to remain irresolute. Greater comfort with and interest in the form of *Don Juan* involves, for these men, transforming *Don Juan* into (virtuous) information; in this respect, they are not far different from the poem's detractors.

The few admiring reviews of *Don Juan* never approve the violation of established poetic principles of form and genre. Byron's supporters may have been less offended by the political and moral content they extracted from the poem, but no reader in any camp recognizes the digressive mode as poetical. To present examples of Byron's poetic talent, reviewers consistently extract those passages which depict a unified action or deliver a self-contained lyric.

The *Literary Museum* says that the "admixture" which has become the dominant mode of Cantos VI–VIII is "more like the

freaks of a petted child than the decided will of a great genius."
The reviewer thus equates weak form with weak will, and goes
on to excerpt, without comment, three of the contrasting passages
that comprise the admixture: the narrator's description of the
Turkish seraglio (VI, 64–66); the skeptical remarks about glory
that close Canto VI (81–87); and the praise for Daniel Boone in
Canto VIII, 61–67 (July 19, 1823, 452–53). He has given up any
search for coherence, and in this respect he resembles the reviewer
for the *Literary Chronicle* who calls Cantos IX–XI a "collection":

> Stanzas that were doled out piecemeal are now collected with
> some additions, and called the 9th, 10th, and 11th cantos of
> this long-winded poem, which may by the same process of
> manufacture be extended to any length. (August 30, 1823,
> 533)

The poet is reduced to a manufacturer of scraps that are not
amenable to critical analysis; readers are at a loss to attach any
artistic function to the poem, admitting that it "holds all the laws
of literature and criticism at defiance" (*Literary Sketch-Book*, December 6, 1823, 258).

Reviewers approve those portions of *Don Juan* directly relevant
to the plot. They are certainly attentive to parts of the poem that
outrage their moral and political sensibilities, but also see their
task as the demonstration of what, after all, makes *Don Juan* art;
to this end, they attempt to show their readers those instances in
which *Don Juan* becomes a fine poem, that is, instances of narrative
coherence.

As the plot thins in the later cantos, many reviewers complain
about their difficulty commenting upon the "poetry" of *Don Juan*.
The *Literary Chronicle* reviewer suggests that his task is just plot
summary when he complains that his "remarks shall be brief as
the incidents they support are scanty" (July 19, 1823, 451). The
Monthly Review prints only the Shooter's Hill passage in its notice
of IX–XI, and has become altogether uninterested in "the usual
digressive style" (October 1821, 218). By the time these cantos
had appeared, readers were treating the poet's digressions as merely
boring. With the appearance of XII–XIV, the *British Critic* writer

gloats about his ability to summarize the plot of all three cantos
into one sentence; he adds that only a dozen or so stanzas are
"not commonplace," and complains that what has become commonplace is "a dry fatiguing desert of cynical twaddle, extending
in cynical sameness through twenty-four hundred and odd lines"
(December 1823, 666). Perhaps the most telling statement comes
in the *Literary Chronicle*, which notes that XII–XIV comprise "a
poem spun out to more than three hundred stanzas, without story,
incident, humor, or satire" and yearns for the poem to manifest
some plot, even an immoral one:

> Some persons . . . think that Lord Byron has formed a regular
> and settled plan for undermining the Christian religion, and
> corrupting public morals. . . . [We] believe that his lordship
> never formed a regular plan for any thing . . . Immorality [in
> *Don Juan*] arises rather from thoughtlessness than design.
> (December 6, 1823, 769)

The poet's immoral viewpoints are considered less offensive
here than an immoral poetics, one which exchanges design for
license. Apparently what Byron's readers wanted was some narrative and descriptive consistency that posited the poet as still
capable of exemplifying "the laws of literature and criticism" even
if he was not always willing to do so. The laws are implied by the
readers' examples of what in the poem is poetical; the "lawful"
passages in *Don Juan* are those poems within the poem that possess
their own lyric, descriptive, or narrative integrity.

An unusual review of Cantos I–II seems almost to admit
what I have attempted to show throughout this discussion, that
poetry is synonymous with information for Byron's readers:

> The defect of *Don Juan* is the same which has been objected
> to in the other works of Lord Byron: much of the interest
> depends on the incidents; and we are apt to ascribe the emo-
> tion with which we are affected in the perusal to the effect of
> the poetry, while it is, in fact, attributable to the surprise that
> we feel in seeing such topics so openly treated. (*Monthly Mag-
> azine*, September 1821, 124–29)

In other words, what readers term poetical or unpoetical corresponds with what they perceive as acceptable or unacceptable information.

I am not arguing that Byron discounts the reality of external facts. His very emphasis upon death, war, bullets, and indigestion insists that there are overwhelming facts and factors that affect us. Also, as Elizabeth Boyd and M. K. Joseph show, *Don Juan* is filled with material from "romance, popular tradition, compendia, satire, novels, memoirs" (Boyd, *et passim*; Joseph, 168). As Jerome McGann has argued, Byron's poem stands apart from the introspective work of other Romantic poets because it is filled with allusions to "history, tradition, and the facts" (155–56). However, what Byron means by facts is different from what I have been calling information. As with each of the pivotal terms in *Don Juan*—war, love, glory, and the rest—the meaning or interpretation of a "fact" cannot be reduced to a customary bit of information.

And yet, "a fact's a fact," inevitable and inescapable. "Fierce loves and faithless wars" are the stuff of human history, and by packing his narrative with historical and literary references Byron shows that human imagination is not, as Wordsworth would have it, the "exertion" of a single mind, but rather the integration of events into consciousness. With persistent references to events outside poetry, *Don Juan* reveals that the truth about the world is 1) not plain and 2) a function of the imaginative freedom which each of us allows himself. The poet's business is not to deny facts, but to expand a repertory of relationships among which facts resonate:

> For checkered as is seen our human lot
> 　　With good, and bad, and worse, alike prolific
> Of melancholy merriment, to quote
> 　　Too much of one sort would be soporific;—
> Without, or with, offense to friends or foes,
> I sketch your world exactly as it goes. (VIII, 89)

The motto for *Don Juan*, "Difficile est propria communia dicere" ("It is difficult to speak of common things in an appropriate manner"), suggests that by fully revealing the context which informs common life, telling "what's what in fact," one risks offending propriety, "that virtuous plough/Which skims the surface" (XII, 40). Propriety generates what I have been calling information, those stiff, thoughtless assumptions which are for Byron a kind of fiction. Moral and political maxims, along with any summary treatment of human behavior, are not facts because they ignore experiential complexity and reduce life to fictive simplicity. By stressing that *Don Juan* has facts, the poet assures a misreading by those who identify facts with appropriate information and at the same time challenges his readers to match his uncommon curiosity and imaginative freedom by rethinking their own belief that "a fact's a fact."

With his medley of facts, Byron aims to present "truths that you will not read in the gazettes." And ironically, the gazettes construe the truth of *Don Juan* so that the poem comes to represent no more than a bit of news, news about the poet's waning powers of imaginative control and precision and his increasing disdain for the prevailing moral, political, and poetical laws. The poem is reduced to a summary of narrative events and authorial transgressions; it becomes a piece of information not too different from the sort of "advertisement" Byron satirizes repeatedly in the poem, one that evokes very little public introspection, regarded instead as a bit of storytelling or scandal whose long-lasting effect is negligible: "ere the ink be dry, the sound grows cold."

That the poem received as much attention from the press as it did has everything to do with the consistent public curiosity about Byron the man or legend; a regard for the poem as biographical information runs through all the reviews. Byron's moral stances are measured against the rumors of his own social escapades, and his political attitudes become inseparable from his real life political activities. Of course, Byron indeed wrote himself into the poem, so biographical conclusions are not unwarranted. But fascination with Byron's life revealed in *Don Juan* is certainly another element of the public penchant for information. Focus on the reckless *persona* behind the words reduces the poem to a kind of diary and necessarily deflects attention from the subtleties of form and expression that make *Don Juan* more a biography of the imagination than the expose of a famous personality.

In several ways, then, Byron's *Don Juan* was accorded the

status of a mere item. Such treatment shrinks the poem to something readable; that is, a piece in which poetry and raving, virtue
and vice, patriotism and treason, are cleanly distinguished and
efficiently judged. We never encounter a reader hard put to draw
conclusions, or one who wonders about the poem as a species of
truth more complicated than any maxim. H. L. Hunt almost reaches
the point of seeing the poem as a complex of meanings; in a review
of Cantos XII–XIV, he reflects on the poet's apparent discovery
"that unalloyed enjoyment is not for any stage of human existence"
and goes on to consider some implications of this idea:

> It is possible enough to be convinced that it is a wise provision
> not to make man too satisfied with a state which he must
> necessarily resign. At all events, it is clear, that the leading
> ranks of life are not exempt from the general discontent of
> humanity; and that, in the midst of abundance, satiety eats
> a rust into their souls. The affections supply the purest sources
> of human satisfaction; and here it is evident that the two
> extremes of society are less fortunate than the grades which
> lie between them. But enough: this is running away without
> a license from *Don Juan*, something too much in the way of
> the noble author, whose possession of one is undeniable.
> (*Literary Examiner*, November 22, 1823)

As he begins to pile up observations that threaten to go out of
control, Hunt checks himself and returns to a more summary
analysis; he will not give himself "license" for the sort of free
association common in *Don Juan*. So even this most liberal reviewer
equates his job with resolute and perspicuous conclusions and
defines the act of reading *Don Juan* as the formation of disciplined
judgments.

DeQuincey, *Essays on Rhetoric and Style*

> The rhetorician's art in its glory and power has silently faded
> away before the stern tendencies of the age; and, if, by any
> peculiarity of taste or strong determination of the intellect,
> a rhetorician *en grande costume* were again to appear amongst

us, it is certain that he would have no better welcome than a stare of surprise as a posturemaker or balancer, not more elevated in the general estimate, but far less amusing, than the acrobat, or funambulist, or equestrian gymnast. No; the age of Rhetoric, like that of Chivalry, has passed among forgotten things.

"Rhetoric," 1828

For Thomas DeQuincey, to practice rhetoric is "to hang upon one's own thoughts as an object of conscious interest, to play with them, to watch and pursue them through a maze of inversions, evolutions, and harlequin changes" (*Selected Essays*, 97; subsequent quotations from this edition). Such rhetoric finds an audience among those willing to share the free play of the mind that the rhetor exploits. But DeQuincey holds little hope that the promise of excursive, speculative discourse will lure anyone away from the instant pleasure of "daily novelties" and the urgency of "public business": "So multiplied are the modes of intellectual enjoyment in modern times that the choice is absolutely distracted; and in a boundless theatre of pleasure, to be had at little or no cost of intellectual activity, it would be marvellous indeed if any considerable audience could be found for an exhibition which presupposes a state of tense exertion on the part of both auditor and performer" (97).

DeQuincey's appreciation for "a state of tense exertion" in reading and writing resonates against the popular advice from Blair's *Lectures*:

> We are pleased with an author, we consider him as deserving praise, who frees us from all fatigue of searching for his meaning; who carries us through his subject without embarrassment or confusion; whose style flows always like a limpid stream, where we see to the very bottom. (I, 186)

For DeQuincey, the "elegant but desultory" Blair represents the "mechanic system," rhetoric reduced to perspicuity and ornament, rhetoric which panders to a society that aggrandizes communicative efficiency, that dismisses the language of patient exploration and speculation as wasteful, "as pure foppery and trifling with time" (100, 192–93).

An early estimate of DeQuincey's contribution to rhetoric was voiced by David Masson in his 1890 comment on DeQuinccy's 1828 essay, "Rhetoric": "Indeed, from the point of view of previous tradition respecting the business of rhetoric, the title of the paper is to a considerable extent a misnomer" (DeQuincey's *Collected Writing* X, 2). Scarcely a handful of essays over the last sixty years oppose Masson's assessment by trying to legitimize DeQuincey's work as a rhetorical theory. Only Paul Talley's 1965 piece and Marie Secor's more recent summary of DeQuincey's theory of style acknowledge the value of his radical view. The lack of appreciation for DeQuincey's rhetorical theory attests to the power of tradition to delimit importance, and sustains Masson's remark as the prevailing view. René Wellek offers a strong and influential voice against the practice of redefining established terms when he declares that DeQuincey's "Rhetoric" has merely "wrenched an acceptable term into a new meaning" (III, 113).

Along with an adherence to tradition goes the suspicion of intellectual play whose end seems to be personal pleasure and novelty only, a suspicion lurking behind the remarks of Masson and Wellek. DeQuincey invites this suspicion with his characterization of rhetoric as play with one's own thought, and especially when he writes elsewhere that "to think reasonably upon any question has never been allowed by me as a sufficient ground for writing upon it, unless I believed myself able to offer some considerable novelty" (*Collected Writing* IV, 2). Stressing the word "offer" in this remark, I think we have a key to DeQuincey's importance. Whatever novelty he achieves stands as an offer that reaches outside the rhetor's fanciful mind and aims at social consequences, the activity of novelty within a community of rhetors who are also citizens and friends. Creating such a community means eschewing definitions and concepts which compartmentalize thought and isolate individuals one from another.

DeQuincey's rhetorical theory emerges from four essays on language (collected in *Selected Essays*): "Rhetoric" (1828), "Style" (1840–41), "Language" (date unknown), and "Conversation" (1847). He begins "Rhetoric" by rejecting popular definitions:

Here then we have in popular use two separate ideas of rhetoric: one of which is occupied with the general end of the fine arts—that is to say, intellectual pleasure; the other applies itself more specifically to a definite purpose of utility, viz. fraud. (82)

In one view, rhetoric is the art of ornament; in the other, the art of persuasion. Rhetoric as ornament stresses the *manner* of presentation; rhetoric as persuasion stresses the *matter*, the content of arguments devised "to dash maturest counsels and to make the worse appear the better reason." Setting aside for a time DeQuincey's emphasis on the dishonesty attendant to persuasion, we might summarize his distinction in classical terms by labeling the rhetoric of ornament as style and the rhetoric of persuasion as invention.

DeQuincey rejects these two views of rhetoric and offers a third "which excludes both." However, he does not really exclude both views; rather, he rejects their designation as *separate* processes, arguing throughout his essays on language that manner and matter, style and invention, become one in the act of a "moving intellect." One of his most explicit arguments against the division of style from invention comes in the essay "Language":

> Now, these offices of style are really not essentially below the level of those offices attached to the original discovery of *truth*. . . . Light to see the road, power to *advance along* it —such being amongst the promises and proper functions of style, it is a capital error, under the idea of ministeriality, to undervalue this great organ of the advancing intellect. . . . The vice of that appreciation which we English apply to style lies in representing it as a mere ornamental accident of written composition—a trivial embellishment, like the mouldings of furniture, the cornices of ceilings, or the arabesques of tea urns. (261)

Agreeing with Wordsworth that style is the *incarnation* rather than the "dress" of thoughts, DeQuincey criticizes the British tendency to "set the matter above the manner"; this "gross mechanical separation" sterilizes both matter and manner and severely limits one's ability to voice more than "external facts, tangible realities, and circumstantial details" (227), predetermined data extraneous to the resources of the intellect. Without the inclination or ability to at once invent and compose thought, an orator cannot think on his feet, and a writer cannot move beyond the facile and commonplace; he cannot "modulate out of one key into the other" (229). One who recognizes that the manner of composition *creates* matter is more able to keep thinking, talking, speculating; and that recognition coincides with tapping one's subjective sensibilities, calling forth the "internal and individual." Only to the degree that one allows subjectivity its exercise "does the style or the embodying of the thoughts cease to be a mere separable ornament" and take on the quality of the moving intellect (229). Rhetoric consists of style which exhibits the confluence of manner and matter as it plays through the possibilities for exploring a subject; DeQuincey recognizes that *conviction* is anathema to restless, shifting queries: "Where conviction begins, the field of rhetoric ends" (82).

Rhetoric's energy is "elliptical," illustrating the rhetor's own labyrinthine movement of mind, and significantly, the polymorphous shape of reflective and fanciful discourse corresponds to the act of reasoning: "All reasoning is carried on discursively; that is, *discurrendo*—by running about to the right and the left, laying the separate notices together, and thence mediately deriving some third apprehension" (103). The dialectical pattern of the rhetor does not conform to the neat lines of a thesis-antithesis-synthesis, much less the linear march through a causal chain, but instead derives new conclusions from the activity of "running about." This mode suits not only the variegated play of subjectivity informing the manner of rhetoric, but also the indeterminate questions which comprise the matter: "Whatsoever is certain, or matter of fixed science, can be no subject of the rhetorician: where it is possible for the understanding to be convinced, no field is open for rhetorical persuasion" (90–91).

DeQuincey mentions his affinity with Aristotle as he acknowledges the power of rhetoric for developing a probable truth and admits that rhetorical expression can involve stressing only one side of an issue and "withdrawing the mind so steadily from all thoughts or images which support the other as to leave it practically under the possession of a one-sided estimate" (91). With intellectual dexterity, the rhetor may so fully exploit his bias that a "mob" of auditors is razzle-dazzled into his camp: "Like boys who are throwing the sun's rays into the eyes of a mob by means of a mirror, you must shift your lights and vibrate your reflections at every possible angle, if you would agitate the popular mind excessively" (139). This statement both acknowledges the stubborn fixity of the popular mind and suggests the licentious potential of rhetorical skill; in view of this potential, DeQuincey offers the curious remark that a licentious technique should be viewed as the "just style in respect of those licentious circumstances," suggesting that the dull-witted auditors deserve what they get (140).

However, the invention of a richly supported bias is only a portion of the rhetorical process, whose fullest expression demonstrates a habit of analogical thinking which does not limit the scope of the understanding. Edmund Burke stands as DeQuincey's hero in this regard:

> All hail to Edmund Burke, the supreme writer of his century, the man of the largest and finest understanding. . . . His great and peculiar distinction was that he viewed all objects of the understanding under more relations than other men, and under more complex relations. According to the multiplicity of these relations, a man is said to have a *large* understanding; according to their subtlety, a *fine* one; and in an angelic understanding all things would appear to be related to all. (115)

The supreme composition spirals outward with "progress and motion, everlasting motion," generated by the rhetor "morbidly impatient of tautology" (129). And rhetoric fully exercised does not encourage blind adherence, but rather, full participation in the art of wondering, that "state of tense exertion on the part of both auditor and performer."

DeQuincey distinguishes oratory from writing enough to suggest the ways in which the prevalent style of the former taints that of the latter and lessens popular appreciation for the complexity of prose rhetoric: *"The modes of style appropriate to popular eloquence being essentially different from those of written composition*, any possible experience on the hustings, or in the senate, would *pro tanto* tend rather to disqualify the mind for appreciating the more chaste and more elaborate qualities of style fitted for books" (141).

The practice of setting the "matter above the manner," using style to merely ornament content, prevails in oratory partly because of the "licentious" designs of some orators, but also because the auditors cannot take advantage of "rereading" an oration:

> It is the advantage of a book that you can return to the last page if anything in the present depends on it. But, return being impossible in the case of a spoken harangue, where each sentence perishes as it is born, both the speaker and the hearer become aware of a mutual interest in a much looser style, and a personal dispensation from the severities of abstract discussion. (140)

That looser style is repetitious rather than generative; the orator re-presents the same proposition through "running variations," in order "to mask, by slight differences in the manner, a virtual identity in the substance" (140). And so audiences become conditioned to extract a simple "message," reinforced through repetition, rather than to share a more wide-ranging, less contrived exploration. Thus conditioned, readers approach books as they do speeches, satisfied to apprehend a single thesis echoed through various stylistic devices.

Along with the influence of popular eloquence, the "necessities of public business" contribute to the foreclosure of contemplation and the surrender to facts and maxims. DeQuincey laments the contemporary reduction in philosophical scope that results while each individual struggles with the "agitations of eternal change" which intensify as society becomes more complex. In modern life, the consideration of indeterminate questions disappears and the urgency of "determinate questions of everyday life" takes over:

> Suppose yourself an Ancient Athenian at some customary display of Athenian oratory, what will be the topic? Peace or war, vengeance for public wrongs, or mercy to prostrate submission, national honor and national gratitude, glory and shame, and every aspect of open appeal to the primal sensibilities of man. On the other hand, enter an English Parliament, having the most of a popular character in its constitution and practice that is anywhere to be found in the Christendom

of this day, and the subject of debate will probably be a road
bill, a bill for enabling a coal-gas company to assume certain
privileges against a competitor in oil-gas, a bill for disfran-
chising a corrupt borough, or perhaps some technical point
of form in the Exchequer Bills bill. So much is the face of
public business vulgarized by details. (98)

As science, business, and politics enlarge and aggrandize the objective and concrete, one's interest in considering and questioning
more abstract, basic issues and assumptions weakens, "because the
rights and wrongs of the case are almost inevitably absorbed to an
unlearned eye by the technicalities of the law, or by the intricacy
of the fact" (99). The intellect required to engage in rhetoric *en
grande costume* languishes on a diet of facts and maxims:

> Rhetoric prospered most at a time when science was unborn
> as a popular interest, and the commercial activities of after-
> times were not sleeping in their rudiments. (100)

In an age obsessed with data extraneous to the "subjective exercises
of the mind," rhetorical free play is not an exigency, and neither
is the "conscious valuation of style" characteristic of a rhetor
focused upon the manner in which his prose gives "evanescent,
external projection to what is internal, outline to what is fluxionary,
and body to what is vague"; lack of concern for the personal
import and creative life of language leaves style aside and demonstrates the writer's belief that "the matter tells without any
manner at all" (226–27). And so the popular prose of the age,
written by and for the shareholders of public business, reveals scant
attention to craft:

> Whatever words tumble out under the blindest accidents of
> the moment, these are the words retained; whatever sweep
> is impressed by chance upon the motion of a period, that is
> the arrangement ratified. (142)

Faced with the bulky periodic *surplusage* of careless writers, "every
man who puts a business value on his time slips naturally into a
trick of shorthand reading." And so a nation of turgid writers has

its readers skimming: "an evil of modern growth is met by a modern remedy" (162).

Prose aspiring to the finest abilities of human discourse bodies forth not a stuffing of thoughtless facts, but the human energy of engagement with an open question, energy seeking a community of intellectual exchange. The model for this searching language, this rhetoric, is conversation. DeQuincey's interest in conversation extends throughout the essays on language, and the properties of the best conversation are identical to the properties of the best rhetoric. Citing the British tendency, in speaking and writing, to remain self-absorbed, "tumid and tumultuary," inflexible, De-Quincey proposes that the more lively prose of France results "from the intense adaptation of the national mind to real colloquial intercourse." The French prize the rapid exchange of views, so that each statement in a conversation remains "brief, terse, simple," always open to reciprocation:

> It passes by necessity to and from, backwards and forwards . . . the momentary subject of interest never *can* settle or linger for any length of time in any one individual without violating the rules of the sport, or suspending its movement; inevitably, therefore, the structure of sentences must for ever be adapted to this primary function of communicativeness, and to the necessities . . . of interminable garrulity. (157)

The individual sentences of colloquial intercourse stay short and simple, but interplay among sentences forms the conversation at large, and we might characterize this larger discourse as a continual sentence of growing, changing theses, couched in the rhythm of the communal mind. The interminable garrulity of "flux and reflux, swell and cadence" models the intellectual play of a discourse resisting closure. So conversation and prose rhetoric share common virtues, as we must conclude when DeQuincey exalts Edmund Burke's conversational ability for the same reason that he names Burke a representative master of rhetoric:

> One remarkable evidence of a *specific* power lying hid in conversation may be seen in such writings as have moved by impulses most nearly resembling those of conversation—for

instance, in those of Edmund Burke—such was the prodigious elasticity of his thinking, equally in his conversation and in his writings, the mere act of movement became the principle or cause of movement. Motion propagated motion, and life threw off life. (269–70)

Associational fluency powers conversation, a fluency uncommon to the "bookish" idiom infecting DeQuincey's Britain, but not to rhetoric *en grande costume*.

Discourse that embodies intensity and play arises from a positive liking for human diversity, and faith in the essentially constructive nature of novel possibilities. DeQuincey calls Samuel Johnson a defective conversationalist and rhetor, who shuns wondering and speculation for one reason:

Because he had little interest in man. Having no sympathy with human nature in its struggles, or faith in the progress of man, he could not be supposed to regard with much interest any forerunning symptoms of changes that to him were themselves indifferent. (273)

In DeQuincey's view, the "desponding taint" in Johnson's blood renders him incapable of "the positive and creative" and limits him to inflexible, monotonous pronouncements. Apart from the question whether Johnson deserves such criticism, and Burke such praise, the idea remains that creative power requires a positive interest in the human condition: "From the heart, from an interest of love or hatred, of hope or care, springs all permanent eloquence" (273).

Insulation from a diversity of language and thought blinds a culture to its own disclosure and informs the kind of self-absorption that feeds indifference. DeQuincey recognizes what modern rhetoricians might call entrapment in one's own "observation language": "The eye cannot see itself; we cannot project from ourselves, and contemplate as an object, our own contemplating faculty, or appreciate our own appreciating power" (153). And in the face of this problem, changes in the popular conception and practice of rhetoric are not likely. A people immersed in language which dulls rather than refreshes thought cannot see the limitation of their style, because the usual way of seeing is itself that style, with its attendant deficiencies and manipulative power: "Easily, therefore, it may have happened that, under the constant action and practical effects of a style, a nation may have failed to notice the cause [style itself] *as* the cause" (139). Style creates and restricts content, and so does *expertise*, because it enfranchises privileged and exclusive viewpoints. DeQuincey develops this idea in "A Brief Appraisal of Greek Literature in Its Foremost Pretentions," where he attacks the Greek Scholar who puts "a preposterous value upon the knowledge":

> So it will always be. Those who . . . possess no accomplishment *but* Greek will, of necessity, set a superhuman value upon that literature in all its parts to which their own narrow skill becomes an available key. . . . It is the habit (well-known to psychologists) of transferring of anything created by our own skill, or which reflects our own skill, as if it lay causatively and objectively in the reflecting thing itself, that pleasurable power which in the very truth belongs subjectively to the mind of him who surveys it, from conscious success in the exercise of his own energies. (292–93)

Coincident with the proposal that rhetoric consists of a subjective play that challenges established priorities and received modes of expression, DeQuincey reiterates the necessity for exploding the conventions of manner and matter while he admits our inescapable dependence upon them.

Rhetoric maintains a tension between convention and invention, mechanic and organic, closure and wonder, and one becomes a rhetorical animal through involvement in the process of intellectual play. Following DeQuincey through the "evolutions, inversions, and harlequin changes" of his own prose, we engage in the very rhetoric he conceives. In "Style," DeQuincey continually reminds us that he is exploiting both the desire of readers for perspicuous prose and the capacity of both writers and readers for sustaining the exploration of a subject:

> Reader, you are beginning to suspect us. "How long do we purpose to detain people?" . . . "And *whither* are we going?

towards what object?—which is as urgent a query as *how far.*" ... You feel symptoms of doubt and restiveness ... unless we explain what it is that we are in quest of. ...

We shall endeavor to bring up our reader to the fence, and persuade him, if possible, to take the leap. ... But as we have reason to believe that he will "refuse" it, we shall wheel him round and bring him up to it from another quarter. (190–91)

This essay and others move through contemporary anecdotes, historical surveys, stylistic analyses and critiques, and addresses to the reader largely through apparent digression, through a wandering away from the subject which might be termed more properly a *wandering into* the subject, given the idea of rhetoric that motivates the prose.

And in the individual sentences, this same presentation of a subjective mind in process contributes to our amazed sense of the number and complexity of perspectives the rhetor may compose. Consider, for example, this description of Herodotus about to speak to the Greeks of his extensive foreign travels and of the war with Persia; for DeQuincey, Herodotus epitomizes two characters, a great explorer and a "patriotic historian":

> Now, if we consider how rare was either character in ancient times, how difficult it was to travel where no passport made it safe, where no preparations in roads, inns, carriages made it convenient; that even five centuries in advance of this era, little knowledge was generally circulated of any region unless so far it had been traversed by the Roman legions; considering the vast credulity of the audience assembled, a gulf capable of swallowing mountains, and, on the other hand, that here was a man fresh from the Pyramids and the Nile, from Tyre, from Babylon and the temple of Belus, a traveller who had gone in with his sickle to a harvest yet untouched; that this same man, considered as a historian, spoke of a struggle with which the earth still agitated; that the people who had triumphed so memorably in this war happened to be the same people who were then listening; that the leaders in this glorious war, whose names had already passed into spiritual powers, were

the fathers of the present audience; combining into one picture all these circumstances, one must admit that no such
meeting between giddy expectation and the very excess of
power to meet its most clamorous calls is likely to have
occurred before or since upon this earth. (180)

Here we experience the cumulative effect of associative thinking,
the "flux and reflux, swell and cadence" which results when the
views illuminating an issue, like voices in an intense conversation,
chime one upon another, until the very point of the sentence—
that Herodotus's speech betokened the scope of human history—
becomes inextricable from the threads of time and place that weave
through the fabric. Reading means participation in DeQuincey's
movement of mind; understanding emerges only *through* that movement, and the reader bent on extracting plain information will
find himself thwarted.

AFTERWORD

Rhetoric Is Back: Derrida, Feyerabend, Geertz, and the Lessons of History

The epistemological crisis of this century—the failure of objectivity, Cartesian rationality, and detachment to account for our complicated perception of a world in flux where matters are never settled—has called into question writing that tries to maintain unity, coherence, perspicuity, and certainty, writing that Edward Said has called "preservative" rather than "investigative" ("The Future of Criticism"). Postmodern critical theory "celebrates" uncertainty, upsetting the generic distinctions that tuck literature, science, and social science away from one another; blurring objectivity and subjectivity, fact and fiction, imagination and reality. As Terry Eagleton demonstrates, what counts as a *literary* test, once one begins taking inventory, just cannot be determined (*Literary Theory* 1–16). All texts being equal, so to speak, any genre—a freshman essay, lyric poem, casual conversation, scientific treatise, lab report—is legitimate game for the critic, and each is potentially rich in "symbolic action."

Just as the definition of a literary text has become a multiple choice, so has the nature of criticism. "The main ideal of criticism," to quote Kenneth Burke's long-standing but curiously postmodern proposition, "is to use all that is there to use" (*Philosophy of Literary*

Form 23). Recognizing that no critical determination is either stable or limited, the postmodern critic acknowledges and "plays" with the psychological, cultural, political, epistemological and linguistic variables that enrich and complicate meaning.

In sum, the recent theory and practice of criticism—that is, commentary about a text—has extended both outside traditionally "literary" disciplines and outside the established criterial realm. One practices criticism not by positing "meaning," but by demonstrating the possibilities for multiple perspectives. Thus, postmodern criticism has reinvented the "forgotten" rhetoric that DeQuincey mourns, the art of wondering demonstrated in the specimen texts of Antiquity and continued by the revisionary figures I have presented in this study.

Kenneth Burke is perhaps the first "postmodern" of this century. In 1931 he wrote *Counterstatement* in response to positivistic movements in both science and the arts; there, in his "*Lexicon Rhetoricae*," Burke proposes that form and meaning in discourse are entirely ambiguous phenomena. The critic's task is the exploitation of that ambiguity; toward that end, as Burke writes later, we need "*terms that clearly reveal the strategic spots at which ambiguities necessarily arise*" (*Grammar* xviii). Burke stands alone, through the New Critical middle of this century, as the great complicator of positivistic and "logocentric" criticism and as a performer of those "inversions, evolutions, and harlequin changes" that "eddy about a truth." With a survey of more recent figures in critical theory, I wish to reinforce the postmodern recognition that texts are "rhetorical," in the richest sense of that term (see Eagleton, *Literary Theory* 205ff, and "A Small History of Rhetoric"). Both more celebrated and infamous than Kenneth Burke, Jacques Derrida reigns as the current proponent of textual indeterminacy.

Derrida recognizes the tendency of all discourse systems to circumscribe thought, noting that the Western practice has been, always and everywhere, to *structure* experience, and "above all to make sure that the organizing principle of the structure would limit what we might call the *play* of the structure."[1] In line with Derrida's proposal, we can regard the dominant mode of communicating literary experience, the critical essay, as one type of limited structure; as Keith Fort argues, "In general, we cannot have attitudes toward reality that cannot be expressed in available forms. If, for example, we can only express our relation to literature in the form of the standard critical essay, we can only have an attitude that would result in the proper form" (174). Derrida believes that resisting enclosure by institutionalized structures requires intellectual play by writers who recognize the limitations of their discourse clearly enough to push against them: "In effect, what appears most fascinating in this critical search for a new status of discourse is the stated abandonment of all reference to a *center*, to a *subject*, to a privileged *reference*, to an *origin*, or to an absolute *archia*" (286).

However, complete "decentering," free play equivalent to total anarchy, can never occur, as Derrida explains. All play begins with "the means at hand" and entails to some extent "the necessity of borrowing one's concepts from the text of a heritage" (282–85). By concluding that all play cannot escape "the culture of reference," Derrida counters any misconception of play as solipsistic meandering with his implication that members of a culture can play *together*, able to share new conceptions because they share the received tradition against which the innovator struggles. But Derrida holds little hope for shared play; what prevails are "dreams of deciphering a truth or an origin which escapes play," dreams of achieving certainty. Those who idealize certainty and conviction "turn their eyes away when faced by the as yet unnameable which is proclaiming itself," blind to departures from received ways of knowing and naming (292–93).

The controversy over textual authority has emerged in the philosophy of science, which also opposes the rhetoric of free play to the valorization of truth. Logical positivism and empiricism have been dethroned by both Thomas Kuhn and Paul Feyerabend. Kuhn's position, that scientific progress always results from a "paradigm shift" which discards theories and methods no longer applicable to new problems, has been adapted by historians, sociologists, and educators, among others, as they recognize that what counts as "research" or "discovery" or "progress" in any discipline depends upon the paradigm implicitly espoused by its practitioners. Kuhn has provoked interest in how the virtues and values of any profession are relative, or we might say, rhetorical.

More interesting, more radical, and less well known than Kuhn, Paul Feyerabend disrupts the philosophy of science with the same advocacy of play as methodology that distinguishes Derrida's work. Feyerabend summarizes his argument "Against Method" with the following advice:

> Do not work with stable concepts. Do not eliminate counterinduction. Do not be seduced into thinking that you have at last found the correct description of "the facts" when all that has happened is that some new categories have been adapted to some older forms of thought, which are so familiar that we take their outlines to be the outlines of the world itself. (36)

This advice means to correct the tendency in scientific education to kill the ability of students to think for themselves and make discoveries: "An essential part of the [scientific] training is the inhibition of intuitions that might lead to a blurring of boundaries. A person's religion, for example, or his metaphysics, or his sense of humor must not have the slightest connection with his scientific activity. His imagination is restrained and even his language will cease to be his own" (20). Shackled by a "professional conscience," students and scientists alike proceed by ignoring any variables that upset the uniformity and "objectivity" of their investigation. In uncompromising opposition to a fixed method or fixed theory, whose fixity "arises from too naive a view of man and of his social surroundings," Feyerabend proposes *counterinduction:* "Introducing, elaborating, and propagating hypotheses which are inconsistent either with well-established theories or well-established facts" (26). Explaining that the proliferation of alternative views coincides with a pluralistic society whose people share their unique talents and predispositions, and that such pluralism flourishes only in the absence of constraints, Feyerabend offers a single maxim: "Anything goes" (26).

Feyerabend's professed "anarchistic theory" does not lead to chaos; he deflects the fear that "anything goes" promotes erosion of all community by stressing the essentially constructive nature of play. With repeated references to the "aimless wandering" of young children engaged in intuitive exploration, he notes that the absence of some predetermined goal or purpose makes possible "accidental solutions to unrealized problems" while the investigator pursues unsanctioned lines of research. And he adds that "we need not fear that the diminished concern for law and order in science and society that is entailed by the anarchistic philosophies will lead to chaos. The human nervous system is too well-organized for that" (21). Even the most "unreasonable, nonsensical, unmethodical" play will tend toward a resolution because each of us cannot tolerate a suspended conclusion for very long. Wondering does lead to a determination, whose consequences need not remain strictly private:

> It is possible to *retain* what one might call the freedom of artistic creation *and to use it to the full*, not just as a road of escape, but as a necessary means for discovering and perhaps even changing the properties of the world we live in. For me this coincidence of the part (individual man) with the whole (the world we live in), of the purely subjective and arbitrary with the objective and lawful, is one of the most important arguments in favor of a pluralistic methodology. (27)

But while recognizing the potential usefulness of the determinations we create, we must not resist their undoing: "Whatever we accept we should trust only tentatively, always remembering that we are in possession, at best, of partial truth (or rightness)" (79). Temporary clarity yields to a fresh start.

One's capacity for innovation varies with the "observation language" one chooses; this major point merges Feyerabend's reflections on science with a theory of the origins and uses of discourse in general and highlights Feyerabend's thinking as a rhetorical theory. He insists that the rhetoric of innovation cannot find voice in the normalized lexicon of old ideas: "We are of course obliged to appeal to the existing forms of speech that do not take [counterinductive speculation] into account and which must be distorted, misused, and beaten into new patterns in order to fit unforeseen situations (without a constant misuse of language there cannot be any discovery and any progress)" (25). Both Derrida and Feyerabend admit the danger of thinking with language that embodies rationalistic and positivistic biases and thus delimits what we are capable of observing, feeling, knowing, changing. They also charge that *any* language, any "style" of investigation, embodies some bias. Such biases are not strictly personal; we carry with us all the cultural and academic and historical baggage that necessarily informs our learning and comprises the context within which we perceive anything. So even deconstructing one's heritage begins with "borrowing" and working with "the means at hand," those very concepts, that very language, one aims to obliterate. Derrida maintains that "no one can escape this necessity" and shares Feyerabend's belief that "experience arises *together with* theoretical assumptions, *not* before them" (Feyerabend 292; Derrida 93).

A certain security comes from the fact that one always begins within a context of "received" assumptions, the security that every "counterinduction" derives somehow from "the culture of reference," and for this reason the innovator sustains a dialogue as well as a tension with that culture, never cut loose altogether from communal exchange, never isolated in an entirely private subjective world. But also, never capable of "pure" observation, only of seeing things in some measure as others have seen them.

Acknowledging the fraudulence of "neutral" perspectives in social anthropology, Clifford Geertz joins forces with Derrida and Feyerabend as he advocates "thick description," an approach set against the practices of "universalizing" the concept of culture, practices which ignore the "piled up structures of inference and implication" that complicate social life. Seeking to "limit, specify, focus, and contain" the concept of culture, modern anthropology has created a "conceptual morass" of vague definitions that "obscures a good deal more than it reveals." Geertz sets out "in search of meaning" rather than "in search of law," with the assumption that meaningful generalizations come from analyzing a very specific situation on a number of levels.

"Thick description" means "doing ethnography," which means doing whatever multiplies the available perspectives: "establishing rapport, selecting informants, transcribing texts, taking genealogies, mapping fields, keeping a diary, and so on" (4–5).[2] Ethnographic research views each culture as a context of interrelationships that can be explicated with the help of heuristic inventories. Del Hymes proposes such an inventory:

For what has to be inventoried and related in an ethnographic account, a somewhat elaborated version of factors identified in communication theory and adapted to linguistics by Roman Jakobson . . . can serve. Briefly put, 1) the various kinds of participants in communicative events—senders and receivers, addressors and addressees, interpreters and spokesmen, and the like; 2) the various available channels and their modes of use: speaking, writing, printing, drumming, blowing, whistling, singing, face and body motion as visually perceived, smelling, tasting, and tactile sensation; 3) the various codes shared by various participants: linguistic, paralinguistic, kinesic, musical, interpretative, interactional, and other; 4) the settings (including other communication) in which communication is permitted, enjoined, encouraged, abridged; 5) the forms of messages, and their genres, ranging verbally from single-morpheme sentences to the patterns and diacritics of sonnets, sermons, salesmen's pitches, and any other organized routines and styles; 6) the attitudes and contents that a message may convey and be about; 7) the events themselves, their kinds and characters as wholes—all these must be identified in an adequate way. (Hymes, *Foundations* 10)

The spirit of free play informs the ethnographic process, insofar as ethnographers deliberately resist "the study of abstracted categories" and counter an ossified observation language with a generative one.

Geertz encourages ethnography while also warning that the fullness, or thickness, of an ethnographic account does not safeguard its accuracy. Because anthropologists always begin observation with conscious and unconscious assumptions and presuppositions, always detached from the native experience itself, "anthropological writings are themselves interpretations, and second and third order ones to boot" (15). To say that all writing interprets rather than re-presents experience threatens "the objective status of anthropological knowledge," as long as we believe that the goal of the process is closure, "discovering the continent of meaning and mapping out its bodiless landscape" (20). But Geertz desires that cultural knowledge become a much more tentative and lively enterprise: "guessing at meanings, assessing the guesses, and drawing explanatory conclusions from the better guesses" (20). The resulting science draws its life from intellectual free play, "marked less by a perfection of consensus than by refinement of debate. What gets better is the precision with which we vex each other" (29).

With summary attention to Derrida, Feyerabend, and Geertz, I have tried to portray an emergent, interdisciplinary critical theory, fundamentally a theory of discourse that devalues certainty and closure while it celebrates the generative power of the imagination. Kenneth Burke reminds us that the proponents and practitioners of postmodern critical theory, with their acute sense of the relativism and ambiguity of every statement, are our rhetoricians:

> A rhetorician, I take it, is like one voice in a dialogue. Put several such voices together, with each voicing its own special assertion, let them act upon one another in co-operative competition, and you get a dialectic that, properly developed, can lead to the views transcending the limitations of each. ("Rhetoric—Old and New," in Steinmann, *New Rhetorics* 63).

Burke recognizes that rhetoric partakes from and contributes to the many voices of social inquiry and equates rhetoric with "identification," social cohesion that results when a multiplicity of views interact. Intellectual movements that follow Burke's conception of rhetoric validate it; postmodernism leaves the suasory dominion of "truth" for the variegated mind-scape of tentative speculation.

Although pluralism and disdain for positivism are fermenting critical theory, institutionalized communicative efficiency prevails outside the pages of postmodernism, where the appointment book is the primary text, individual achievement and happiness are all, progress is linear, and the universe exists in binary permutations of a silicon chip. It is, or it isn't. In the academy, the numbers and diversity of our students continue to increase, and that diversity is threatened by both the standardization of literacy and competency and the appeal of a marketplace that pays for hard data and speedy conclusions.

My revisions in the history of rhetoric mean to question the prominent virtues informing traditional and conventional attitudes about literacy. In even the most enlightened composition class, a class blown by the winds of change through a "paradigm shift" into a student-centered, process-oriented environment replete with heuristics, sentence combining, workshopping, conferencing, and recursive revising, speculation and exploration remain subordinate to finishing. Certainly, learning to write in such a class may be a richer and more interesting enterprise than before, because "process" has upstaged "product"; pages about prewriting and rewriting now appear in composition textbooks. But while classrooms and textbooks give more time and attention to process (that is, "unfinished" writing), work-in-process does not count as writing, at least not as writing that counts.

What counts, if we survey writing competency exams (which, after all, represent a prevailing definition of rhetoric and writing) is rushing through the beginning, middle, and end of an uncontemplated and patently artificial topic in 30 or 40 minutes. The student writer's movement of mind among ideas, facts, and possibilities is beside the point when representative measures of competency obtain (Covino, "Writing Tests and Creative Fluency").

What counts is ending rather than continuing the discourse. And even in the process-busy classroom, what counts when all the prewriting and revising ends is some type of academic essay, some demonstration of all the virtues of mainstream literacy—unity, coherence, perspicuity, closure, and correctness. Because the academic essay is the end of the composing process, both on exams and in classrooms, and because closing a discourse counts more than the questions and qualifications that keep discourse open, the emphasis our discipline has placed on the composing process over the last dozen years, especially on the plurality of processes available to writers, remains ironic. While writing is identified exclusively with a product and purpose that contain and abbreviate it, writers let the conclusion dictate their tasks and necessarily censor whatever imagined possibilities seem irrelevant or inappropriate; they develop a trained incapacity to speculate and raise questions, to try stylistic and formal alternatives. They become unwilling and unable to fully elaborate the process of composing.

Without minimizing the importance of making up one's mind, or of creating a finished document, and with appreciation for the utility and beauty of cogent prose, I question the overriding preference for a closed form as the token of literacy. And I call for a philosophy of composition that exploits writing as a mode of *avoiding* rather than *intending* closure, a philosophy of composition informed by the lessons of a revisionist history, a philosophy of composition that exploits writing as philosophy.

I have in mind a student writing whose model is Montaigne or Byron or DeQuincey or Kenneth Burke or Tom Wolfe, a student for whom, as Henry Miller says, "there is no progress: there is perpetual movement, displacement, which is circular, spiral, endless" (180). The writing is informed by associational thinking, a repertory of harlequin changes, by the resolution that resolution itself is anathema. This writer writes to see what happens.

I am not suggesting that students should learn to trade clarity for obscurity (a trade that some postmodern writers have been accused of making). I am suggesting that they should trade certainty for ambiguity, trade preservative writing for investigative writing, trade conclusions for "counterinduction." The climate is right for writing teachers to point out that the world is a drama of people and ideas and that writing is how we consistently locate and relocate ourselves in the play.

What writers must maintain is thoughtful uncertainty, the attitude that necessarily informs full exploration and motivates wonder. That attitude is proof against the notion that writing proficiency necessarily involves a "haste to score, to make a quick intellectual killing" (Moffett 140) and, furthermore, proof against the narcissism that may be the most outstanding and disabling epidemic of this decade. As Christopher Lasch points out, the "narcissistic personality of our times" is one for whom creativity is a "success formula" used for self-aggrandizement rather than for enriching one's sense of interdependence (71–103). And Arthur Levine's study of college students concludes that "Today, students are playing to win, take whatever they can get, and then push for more" (50).

Thoughtful uncertainty seems neither profitable nor fashionable. But it is uncertainty that provokes the investigation of possibilities beyond one's stock response; uncertainty necessarily sends us into conversation with other ideas and people. As Kenneth Burke has pointed out through all of his work, the longer we can maintain this conversation and forestall taking a stance, the longer we avoid the conflict, intolerance, and oppression informed by ossified viewpoints.

While the intellectual and political foundations and implications of open discourse are intricate, the way to encourage such discourse in the academy is simple: just make it count. Then, a thick folder of "sustained invention" is more important than a short stack of themes; then, legitimate classroom genres are dialogue and drama, forms that enfranchise the interplay of viewpoints; then, an apparent fact such as "Romeo and Juliet are in love" prompts us to consider whether love, both inside and outside Shakespeare's play and milieu, is really hate, or lust, or greed, or rashness, or empty verbiage, or a kind of murder or suicide, or loyalty, or absolute unselfishness, or the nectar of the gods, or fate. Then, puzzlement and disequilibrium are the elements of rhetoric.

Notes

Chapter One. The Classical Art of Wondering: Plato, Aristotle, Cicero

1. "Introductions" to classical rhetoric typically schematize and simplify classical texts. See, for instance, xxv–1i of the Freese translation of Aristotle's *Rhetoric*; George Kennedy's *Classical Rhetoric* 69; Golden's *The Rhetoric of Western Thought* 52, 65–72.

2. See especially several essays in Conners (ed.), *Classical Rhetoric and Modern Discourse*: Andrea Lunsford and Lisa Ede, "On Distinctions Between Classical and Modern Rhetoric" 37–49; Frank D'Angelo, "The Evolution of the Analytic *Topoi*: A Speculative Inquiry" 50–68; John Gage, "An Adequate Epistemology for Composition" 152–69. Also, see Janet Emig's 1982 summary conclusion that "Within the past fifteen years rhetoricians have focused primarily on invention and secondarily upon style," in "Writing, Composition, and Rhetoric," *Encyclopedia of Educational Research* 2023.

3. Hugh Blair's understanding of Quintilian's first-century *Institutio Oratoria* informs his identification of rhetoric with perspicuous style in the eighteenth-century *Lectures on Rhetoric and Belles-Lettres*; Thomas Wilson's sixteenth-century *Arte of Rhetorique* is one of the first "Ciceronian" rhetorics to appear in English; Theophrastus was the student of Aristotle who is credited with interpreting and reorganizing the *Rhetoric* for use in Hellenistic schools.

4. Hunt's summary, first published in a shorter version in the 1920 *Quarterly Journal of Speech*, has appeared since then as part of his "classic article on the views of Plato and Aristotle concerning rhetoric" (Enos 1980, 29) which "endures as required reading for students of classical rhetoric" (Enos 1983, 25). Golden features Hunt's summary in *The Rhetoric of Western Thought* 50–51. Hunt's

complete essay is reprinted in Drummond 3–60 and Howes 19–70.

5. Citations for the *Phaedrus* refer to section numbers, as given in the Helmbold and Rabinowitz translation.

6. As George Kennedy concludes, the "major problem" with Socrates' summary is "the practical one": "How can an orator know the souls of his audience in any full sense? And if he does, how can he fit his speech to the variety of souls likely to be found there? How can he keep from enflaming one at the same time he calms another?" (*Classical Rhetoric* 58–59). Socrates' preference for speaking with individuals rather than to groups does not mitigate the impossibility of addressing "every changing mood of the complicated soul."

7. Robert Connors' recent assessment of Plato's "open hostility toward writing" emphasizes that Plato's "arguments against writing are tinged more with contempt than with passion" and that, for Plato, writing is "to be repudiated by a seeker of truth" ("Greek Rhetoric and Orality" 54–55).

8. Other standard translations maintain the sense of the phrase "in a way": in Hackforth, "the discussion that engaged us may be said to have concerned love"; in Cooper, "the subject we discussed was, in its way, the subject of Love"; in Jowett, "the theme which occupied us was love—after a fashion."

9. This is George Kennedy's paraphrase/translation of 1140a, 10–15; see *Classical Rhetoric* 62. In correspondence with me Professor Kennedy has explained his translation as an acknowledgment of an earlier proposition in the *Ethics*: that the poetic and practic (i.e., art) belong in the category of that which is capable of being other than (or different from) what it is.

10. Throughout *De Oratore*, Cicero refers to the art of *eloquence*, the study of *rhetoric*, and the presentation of *oratory* without distinguishing categorically among these terms; thus, he reinforces the ambiguity of his rhetorical theory. I will treat *eloquence* and *rhetoric* as roughly synonymous terms in this discussion, mindful that they are not so always and everywhere.

11. George Kennedy notes that "the historicity of the dialogue has been doubted" in *The Art of Rhetoric in the Roman World* 215n.

12. Ralph Micken points out that "it is usually assumed that Crassus speaks for Cicero and Antonius for brother Quintus. This is, however, a division that can be overstressed. As we have said elsewhere, Antonius must certainly represent Marcus Cicero on the subject of invention, and Julius Caesar Vopiscus is surely the author's spokesman on the subject of humor" (Introduction to *On Oratory and Orators* xxxv).

Chapter Two. Knowledge as Exploration: Montaigne, Vico, Hume

1. Golden accurately notes (132) that Descartes' work (primarily the 1637 *Discourse on Method*) "influenced the direction and thrust of the French Academy and, indeed, became a textbook for the Port-Royal logicians and rhetoricians who, in turn, influenced British thought."

   In a note to his translation of Vico's *Study Methods*, Gianturco emphasizes the decidedly non-Vichian character of Descartes' definition of method in the *Rules for the Direction of the Mind:* "a set of certain and easy rules, such that anyone who obeys them exactly, will, first, never take anything false for true, and secondly, will advance step by step, without waste of mental effort, until he has achieved the knowledge of everything which does not surpass his capacity of understanding" (*Study Methods* 6–7n).
2. My initial understanding of Vico's *Study Methods* is much indebted to John Schaeffer, "Vico's Rhetorical Model of the Mind: *Sensus Communis* in *De nostri temporis studiorum ratione.*"
3. This is Schaeffer's translation, more appropriate in this case than Gianturco's. See Schaeffer 157 and 166n.
4. In his discussion of Vico's late essay, *On the Heroic Mind*, Mooney concludes that Vico "celebrates discovery as surprise, as the almost random conjunction of accident and genius" (99).

Chapter Three. The Psychology of Reading: Blair, Byron, DeQuincey

1. Periodical reviews of Byron's works are photocopied in Reiman, *The Romantics Reviewed.*
2. In *Byron: A Poet Before His Public*, Philip Martin skirts his promise to explicate the presuppositions of Byron's readers, but does correctly propose that any critic of *Don Juan* "projects into it themes and contexts" (173).

Afterword. Rhetoric Is Back:
Derrida, Feyerabend, Geertz,
and the Lessons of History

1. The particular critical search to which Derrida refers is that of Lévi-Strauss in *The Raw and the Cooked*, whose method Derrida admires and engages in himself, with differences.

   All quotations by Derrida are from the seminal presentation of his philosophy, "Structure, Sign, and Play in the Discourse of the Human Sciences."

2. All quotations from Geertz are from "Thick Description" in *The Interpretation of Cultures*; Geertz further elaborates thick description and the postmodern tendency toward "blurred genres" in *Local Knowledge*.

Works Cited

Aristotle. *The "Art" of Rhetoric*. Trans. J. H. Freese. Cambridge: Harvard UP, 1926.

——. *The Rhetoric of Aristotle*. Trans. Lane Cooper. Englewood Cliffs, NJ: Prentice-Hall, 1932.

Arrington, Philip K. "Tropes of the Composing Process." *College English* 48 (April 1986): 325–38.

Ayer, A. J. *Hume*. New York: Hill and Wang, 1980.

Bacon, Francis. *The Advancement of Learning*. Ed. G. W. Kitchin. Totowa, NJ: Rowman and Littlefield, 1973.

Bennett, Jonathan. *Locke, Berkeley, Hume: Central Themes*. Oxford: Clarendon, 1971.

Blair, Hugh. *Lectures on Rhetoric and Belles-Lettres*. Ed. Harold F. Harding. 2 vols. Carbondale: Southern Illinois UP, 1965.

Blakesley, David. "Manner as Form in Aristotle's *Rhetoric*. Unpublished thesis. San Diego State University, 1986.

Boyd, Elizabeth. *Byron's* Don Juan. 1945. New York: Humanities, 1958.

Burger, Ronna. *Plato's* Phaedrus: *A Defense of the Philosophic Art of Writing*. University: U of Alabama P, 1980.

Burke, Kenneth. *Counterstatement*. 2nd ed. 1953. Berkeley: U of California P, 1968.

——. *A Grammar of Motives*. 1945. Berkeley: U of California P, 1969.

——. *The Philosophy of Literary Form*. 3rd ed. Berkeley: U of California P, 1973.

Byron, George Gordon, Lord. *Don Juan*. Ed. Leslie A. Marchand. Boston: Houghton Mifflin, 1958.

Bywater, Ingram. Introduction. *Poetics*. By Aristotle. Oxford: Clarendon, 1909.

Charvat, William. *The Origins of American Critical Thought, 1810–1835*. Philadelphia: U of Pennsylvania P, 1936.

Cicero. *De Inventione*. Trans. H. M. Hubbell. Cambridge: Harvard UP, 1949.

————. *De Oratore (On Oratory and Orators)*. Trans. J. S. Watson. Carbondale: Southern Illinois UP, 1970.

————. *De Partitiones Oratoriae*. Trans. H. Rackham. Cambridge: Harvard UP, 1942.

————. *Orator*. Trans. H. M. Hubbell. Cambridge: Harvard UP, 1952.

Clark, M. L. *Rhetoric at Rome*. New York: Barnes & Noble, 1966.

Cohen, Ralph, ed. *The Essential David Hume*. New York: Bantam, 1965.

Connors, Robert J. "Greek Rhetoric and Orality." *Philosophy and Rhetoric* 19:1 (1986): 38–65.

Connors, Robert J., Lisa Ede, and Andrea Lunsford, eds. *Classical Rhetoric and Modern Discourse*. Carbondale: Southern Illinois UP, 1984.

Corbett, Edward P. J. *Classical Rhetoric for the Modern Student*. 2nd ed. New York: Oxford UP, 1971.

Covino, William A. "Writing Tests and Creative Fluency." *Rhetoric Review* 3 (1984): 50–57.

Croll, Morris. "Attic Prose: Lipsius, Montaigne, Bacon." *Style, Rhetoric, and Rhythm*. Ed. J. Max Patrick and Robert O. Evans. Princeton: Princeton UP, 1969. 167–206.

DeQuincey, Thomas. *The Collected Writing of Thomas DeQuincey*. Ed. David Masson. 1890. New York: AMS, 1968.

————. *Selected Essays on Rhetoric*. Ed. Frederick Burwick. Carbondale: Southern Illinois UP, 1967.

Derrida, Jacques. "Structure, Sign, and Play in the Discourse of the Human Sciences." *Writing and Difference*. Trans. Alan Bass. Chicago: U of Chicago P, 1978.

Descartes, René. *Discourse on Method*. Trans. Paul J. Olscamp. Indianapolis: Bobbs-Merrill, 1965.

Drummond, A. M., ed. *Studies in Rhetoric and Public Speaking in Honor of James A. Winans*. New York: Century, 1925.

Eagleton, Terry. *Literary Theory*. Minneapolis: U of Minnesota P, 1983.

————. "A Small History of Rhetoric." *Walter Benjamin, or Towards a Revolutionary Criticism*. London: NLB, 1981. 101–13.

Emig, Janet. "Writing, Composition, and Rhetoric." *Encyclopedia of Educational Research*. New York: Free Press, 1982: 2021–2036.

Enos, Richard Leo. "The Classical Period," *Historical Rhetoric: An Annotated Bibliography*. Ed. Winifred Horner. Boston: Hall, 1980. 1–41.

————. "The Classical Period." *The Present State of Scholarship in Historical and Contemporary Rhetoric*. Columbia: U of Missouri P, 1983. 10–39.

Feyerabend, Paul. *Against Method: Outline of Anarchistic Theory of Knowledge*. *Minnesota Studies in the Philosophy of Science* 4 (1960). New York: Schocken, 1978.

Flesch, Rudolf. *The Art of Readable Writing*. New York: Harper, 1949.

Fort, Keith. "Form, Authority, and the Critical Essay." *Contemporary Rhetoric*. Ed. W. Ross Winterowd. New York: Harcourt, 1975.

Geertz, Clifford. *The Interpretation of Cultures*. New York: Basic, 1973.

————. *Local Knowledge*. New York: Basic, 1983.

Golden, James L., Goodwin Berquist, and William Coleman. *The Rhetoric of Western Thought*. 3d ed. Dubuque: Kendall/Hunt, 1983.

Grassi, Ernesto. *Rhetoric as Philosophy*. University Park: Penn State UP, 1980.

Grieg, J. Y. T., ed. *The Letters of David Hume*. 2 vols. London: Oxford UP, 1932.

Grimaldi, William M. *Studies in the Philosophy of Aristotle's Rhetoric*. Wiesbaden: Franz Steiner Verlag, 1972.

Hill, Forbes I. *The Genetic Method in Recent Criticism on the Rhetoric of Aristotle*. Diss. Cornell U, 1963. Ann Arbor: UMI, 1980. 63–8111.

Howell, Wilbur Samuel. *Logic and Rhetoric in England, 1500–1700*. New York: Russell & Russell, 1961.

Howes, Raymond F. *Historical Studies of Rhetoric and Rhetoricians*. Ithaca: Cornell UP, 1961.

Hume, David. *Philosophical Works*. Ed. T. H. Greene and T. H. Grose. 4 vols. Germany: Scientia Verlag Aalen, 1964.

————. *A Treatise on Human Nature*. Ed. L. A. Selby-Bigge. Oxford: Clarendon, 1888.

Hunt, Everett Lee. "Plato and Aristotle on Rhetoric and Rhetoricians." *Quarterly Journal of Speech* 6 (June 1920): 33–53.

Hymes, Del. *Foundations in Sociolinguistics*. Philadelphia: U of Pennsylvania P, 1974.

Jakobson, Roman. "The Metaphoric and Metonymic Poles." *Critical Theory Since Plato*. Ed. Hazard Adams. New York: Harcourt, 1971.

Joseph, M. K. *Byron the Poet*. London: Oxford UP, 1964.

Kahn, Victoria. *Rhetoric, Prudence, and Skepticism in the Renaissance*. Ithaca: Cornell UP, 1985.

Kennedy, George. *The Art of Rhetoric in the Roman World*. Princeton: Princeton UP, 1972.

————. *Classical Rhetoric and Its Christian and Secular Tradition*. Chapel Hill: U of North Carolina P, 1980.

Knoblauch, C. H. and Lil Brannon. *Rhetorical Traditions and the Teaching of Writing*. Portsmouth, NH: Boynton/Cook, 1984.

Kuhn, Thomas. *The Structure of Scientific Revolutions*. 2nd ed. Chicago: U of Chicago P, 1970.

Lasch, Christopher. *The Culture of Narcissism*. New York: Warner, 1979.

Levine, Arthur. *When Dreams and Heroes Died: A Portrait of Today's College Student*. San Francisco: Jossey-Bass, 1981.

Marchand, Leslie, ed. *Byron's Letters and Journals*. 12 vols. Cambridge: Cambridge UP, 1982.

Martin, Philip W. *Byron: A Poet Before His Public*. Cambridge: Cambridge UP, 1982.

McGann, Jerome J. *Don Juan in Context*. Chicago: U of Chicago P, 1976.

McKeon, Richard D. "The Hellenistic and Roman Foundations of the Tradition of Aristotle in the West." *Review of Metaphysics* 32 (1979): 677–715.

Micken, Ralph. Introduction. *De Oratore (On Oratory and Orators)*. By Cicero. Carbondale: Southern Illinois UP, 1970.

Miller, Henry. "Reflections on Writing," *The Creative Process*. Ed. Brewster Ghiselin. Berkeley: U of California P, 1952. 178–85.

Moffett, James. "Writing, Inner Speech, and Meditation." *Coming on Center*. Portsmouth, NH: Boynton/Cook, 1981.

Montaigne, Michel de. *The Complete Works of Montaigne*. Ed. and Trans. Donald Frame. Stanford: Stanford UP, 1967.

Mooney, Michael. *Vico in the Tradition of Rhetoric*. Princeton: Princeton UP, 1985.

Mossner, Ernest Campbell. *The Life of David Hume*. 2d ed. Oxford: Oxford UP, 1980.

Murphy, James J. *Rhetoric in the Middle Ages*. Berkeley: U of California P, 1974.

Ong, Walter. *Ramus, Method, and the Decay of Dialogue*. Cambridge: Harvard UP, 1958.

Pattison, Robert. *On Literacy: The Politics of the Word from Homer to the Age of Rock*. New York: Oxford UP, 1982.

Pieper, Josef. *Enthusiasm and Divine Madness*. Trans. Richard and Clara Winston. New York: Harcourt, 1964.

Plato, *Phaedrus*. Trans. Lane Cooper. In *Plato*. New York: Oxford UP, 1938. 7–71.

———. *Phaedrus*. Trans. Reginald Hackforth. Cambridge: Cambridge UP, 1972.

———. *Phaedrus*. Trans. W.C. Helmbold and W.G. Rabinowitz. Indianapolis: Bobbs-Merrill, 1956.

———. *Phaedrus*. Trans. B. Jowett. In *The Works of Plato*. New York: Tudor, 1937: III, 359–449.

Popkin, Richard H. *The High Road to Pyrrhonism*. San Diego: Austin Hill, 1980.

Randall, J.H. *Aristotle*. New York: Columbia UP, 1960.

Reiman, Donald H. *The Romantics Reviewed: Contemporary Reviews of British Romantic Writers*. 9 vols. New York: Garland, 1972.

Said, Edward. "The Future of Criticism." Modern Language Association Convention. New York, 29 Dec. 1983.

Schaeffer, John D. "Vico's Rhetorical Model of the Mind: *Sensus Communis* in *De nostri temporis studiorum ratione*." *Philosophy and Rhetoric* 14:3 (1981): 152–67.

Secor, Marie. "The Legacy of Nineteenth-Century Style Theory," *Rhetoric Society Quarterly* 22 (Spring 1982): 76–84.

Solmsen, Frederich. "The Aristotelian Tradition in Ancient Rhetoric." *Aristotle: The Classical Heritage of Rhetoric.* Ed. Keith V. Erickson. Metuchen, NJ: Scarecrow, 1974.

Sprat, Thomas. *History of the Royal Society.* Ed. Jackson Cope and Harold Jones. St. Louis: Washington UP, 1958.

Steinmann, Martin, ed. *New Rhetorics.* New York: Scribner's, 1967.

Talley, Paul. "DeQuincey on Persuasion, Invention, and Style." *Central States Speech Journal* 16 (1965): 243–54.

Valesio, Paolo. *Novantiqua.* Bloomington: Indiana UP, 1980.

Verene, Donald Philip. "The New Art of Narration: Vico and the Muses." *New Vico Studies 1983.* Atlantic Highlands: Humanities, 1983.

———. *Vico's Science of Imagination.* Ithaca: Cornell UP, 1981.

Vico, Giambattista. *The Autobiography of Giambattista Vico.* Trans. Max H. Fisch and Thomas G. Bergin. Ithaca: Cornell UP, 1944.

———. *The New Science.* Trans. Thomas G. Bergin and Max H. Fisch. 2d rev. ed. Ithaca: Cornell UP, 1968.

———. *On the Study Methods of Our Time.* Trans. Elio Gianturco. Indianapolis: Bobbs-Merrill, 1965.

———. *Selected Writings.* Ed. Leon Pompa. Cambridge: Cambridge UP, 1982.

Wagner, Russell. "Wilson and His Sources." *Quarterly Journal of Speech* 15 (1929): 530–32.

Walker, Keith. *Byron's Readers: A Study of Attitudes Toward Byron.* Salzburg: Institut für Anglistik und Amerikanistik, 1979.

Weathers, Winston. *An Alternate Style.* Rochelle Park, NJ: Hayden, 1980.

Weaver, Richard. *The Ethics of Rhetoric.* Chicago: Regnery, 1953.

Wellek, René. *A History of Modern Criticism.* 4 vols. New Haven: Yale UP, 1955.

Whateley, Richard. *Elements of Rhetoric.* Ed. Douglas Eninger, Carbondale: Southern Illinois UP, 1963.

Wilson, Thomas. *Arte of Rhetorique.* Ed. Thomas Derrick. New York: Garland, 1982.